William Alexander Parsons Martin

The Analytical Reader

A Short Method for Learning to Read and Write Chinese

William Alexander Parsons Martin

The Analytical Reader
A Short Method for Learning to Read and Write Chinese

ISBN/EAN: 9783337003760

Printed in Europe, USA, Canada, Australia, Japan

Cover: Foto ©Paul-Georg Meister /pixelio.de

More available books at **www.hansebooks.com**

ANALYTICAL READER.

認

常

A

SHORT METHOD

FOR

字 字

LEARNING TO READ AND WRITE CHINESE,

BY

REV. W. A. P. MARTIN, D. D.

雙 新

OF

THE AMERICAN PRESBYTERIAN MISSION.

———

千 法

SHANGHAI:
PRESBYTERIAN MISSION PRESS.
PUBLISHED BY THE MISSION.
1863.

THE RIGHT OF REPRINTING RESERVED.

PART I.—THE METHOD

For euphony's sake I have called it *Short*; though in strictness, the adjective ought to have been placed in the comparative degree. There is no *positively* short road to an acquaintance with Chinese. But the method explained and illustrated in the following pages proposes, in some measure, to abridge the labor.

This it effects in two ways—

First, by furnishing the student with precisely those characters which he needs to know;

Secondly, by laying them open to the eye, and impressing them on the memory.

In neither of these respects does it lay claim to entire originality, nor is it a doubtful experiment. It treads in a safe path, at the entrance of which the natives have planted finger-boards, though they have not pursued it quite as far as we propose to venture.

They discovered the needle; it was reserved for others to use it in crossing the ocean. They analyze with beautiful simplicity a few scores of family names—we seize the hint and launch into the sea of words, confident that it shows us the *way* to the further shore. They select a thousand characters as a capital for beginners; and with a view to aiding the memory, combine them into verse. We borrow the idea, and duly acknowledging our obligation, proceed, as we believe, to improve upon it. Their thousand were taken at random; we take twice the number, and select them by a regular process which required years of painstaking. They govern the distribution by no laws but those of metre. We too arrange them in verse; but dispose them in such a manner that they are presented to the learner in a steady gradation, according to the frequency of their occurrence. These, and other leading features, require further elucidation.

1. *The Selection of Characters.*

Several years ago I commenced a volume, on a plan somewhat similar to that of the present work. Its progress was interrupted by a voyage to America; but when I returned, I was enabled to resume the task on a better basis. At first I had been guided in the selection of characters by no surer rule than the judgment of a Chinese scribe, who culled them from the pages of K'anghi's Dictionary. I was now favored with a list, formed on scientific principles, in which every character was placed with numerical precision according to the frequency of its use.

For this, I was indebted to Mr. Wm. Gamble, Superintendent of the Presbyterian Mission Press.

Mr. Gamble prepared it for a purpose very different from mine, viz. to ascertain the proportion in which the several letters would be required in casting a font of metallic type; and to determine in what order the types should be arranged, so as to bring those in most common use, nearest to the hand of the compositor. Both of these ends it succeeded in effecting—preventing a waste of metal in casting useless type, and increasing the rapidity of "composition". But it was obvious that a collection arranged with such elaborate care might be adapted to a higher end—to save the time expended in learning rare or useless characters, and abbreviate for foreign students, or Chinese pupils the tedious task of acquiring the written language. The process by which these tables were constructed is well stated by Mr. Gamble, in an "Introduction", the greater part of which I take the liberty of transcribing, for the sake of the information it contains.

"In order to the better understanding of the following lists of selected characters, it is necessary to give some explanation of the manner in which they have been prepared, and of the object which has been kept in view in their preparation.

"When the art of printing first sprung up in the Western world, printers found it necessary to compute the relative frequency with which each letter of the alphabet occurred in order to ascertain how many type of each sort it would be necessary to cast, so that there should not be too many of one letter and too few of another. Thus for ordinary English book work the proportion of each letter in a fount are, of *e* 12000, of *t* 9000, of *a* 8500, of *i n o* and *s*, each 8000, of *r* 6200; while *k* only occurs 800 times, *q* 500, *j* and *x* 400, and *z* but 200. They also in arranging them in cases, placed those that occurred most frequently in adjoining compartments and near the hand of the compositor, for the purpose of thereby promoting rapidity in the composition or *setting up* of the type.

"But in China the use of metallic type has been of such modern date, that little has as yet been done towards ascertaining the relative frequency with which characters occur in the general literature of this peculiar language. This remark holds good even with reference to its christain literature, which is now becoming pretty extensive, and in which those who are engaged in missionary operations are more particularly interested. In consequence therefore of the want of correct data on which to form a *scale*, as printers call it, of the characters in the written language, the method hitherto in use, of arranging founts of Chinese metallic type, has been such that not only have the type themselves taken up much room, but the compositor in going from case to case for each type has unavoidably consumed so much time, as thereby to render composition both expensive and tedious.

"With the view therefore of making some improvement upon the former method of arrangement, as well as of ascertaining how many of the 40919 characters contained in K'ang-hi's Dictionary are in common use, especially in the class of books used and published by those engaged in the Missionary work; an examination was made of 4166 octavo pages; including the whole Bible together with twenty seven other publications printed at our press, and embracing in the aggregate nearly one million two hundred thousand characters. In conducting this examination two Chinese scholars were employed for two years each, and it was carried on in such a manner as to secure as much accuracy as possible. The result is shown in the two following lists.

"The FIRST LIST which is arranged in the usual manner by Radicals and Strokes, contains every character which occurs in the above mentioned books, amounting in number only to 5150 different characters. The number of times each of these characters occurred is placed opposite to it in figures, which when added together show an aggregate of 1166473 characters. It may here be proper to add that in the Scriptures containing the total number of 676827 characters there were found 4141 different ones. In the Old Testament there are in all 503663 characters and 3946 different ones; the version used being that printed at the London Mission press. In the New Testament there are in all 173164 characters and 2713 different ones; the version used being that printed at the Presbyterian Mission press.

"That so few characters are of general use as is shown by this statement may seem somewhat incredible to those who have not examined the subject, and who having been accustomed to hear the number of characters in the Chinese language stated to be forty to eighty thousand, suppose that in order to be able to read or translate Chinese books, a knowledge of some tens of thousands of characters is absolutely necessary. Our calculations are however corroborated by the author of the Chinese work called the 十三經集字

Shih san king tsih ts who states that the 四書 *Four Books* contain 2328 different characters; the 五經 *Five Classics* contain 2426 different characters which do not occur in the *Four Books*, and that the whole number of different characters in the *Thirteen Classics* is 6544. This includes 928 rare or obsolete characters occurring in the 爾雅 *Ready Guide*, almost all of which might be omitted, thus leaving less than 6000 characters.

"The SECOND LIST, like the first one, consists of all the characters different from each other that are to be found in the total number examined, but here it is intended to exhibit them arranged according to their numerical use, or the relative frequency with which they occur. For this purpose they are divided into *fifteen groups*, in each of which is contained all the characters occurring between a certain number of times each, as, between 1000 and 10000 times each, between 900 and 1000 times each, between 800 and 900 times each, and so on of the others. The first group, however, has all those that occurred over 10000 times each; and the fifteenth group includes the 850 mentioned above as taken from another list, which ought properly to be placed in a group by themselves.

"The group—the number of different characters in each group—their minimum and maximum numbers—together with the total number of times that the characters of each group occurred: is shown in the following table:—

Group.	No. Different Cha.	Min. & Max. Nos.	Totals.
1st.	13	10000	214156
2d.	224	1000 –10000	563126
3d.	16	900 – 1000	15150
4th.	19	800 – 900	16344
5th.	44	700 – 800	32757
6th.	47	600 – 700	31167
7th.	59	500 – 600	32116
8th.	99	400 – 500	44258
9th.	112	300 – 400	38024
10th.	197	200 – 300	47932
11th.	400	100 – 200	56627
12th.	207	75 – 100	17637
13th.	301	50 – 75	18508
14th.	547	25 – 50	19497
15th.	3715	1 – 25	19036
	6000		1166335

"As the result of this investigation two most important facts to the printer are established. FIRST: *that five or six thousand well selected characters are sufficient for all practical purposes*; which is, about *one-seventh* of what is in the language. This has been long known in China, but appears to have been overlooked by those interested in such matters in Europe. SECOND: *that a very few characters, from the great frequency with which they occur, constitute the great body of those in a book, and that the great majority occur exceedingly seldom*. Thus, as already stated, the first group has 13 characters which were found to occur in the whole number examined 214156 times, which is more than *one-sixth* of the whole. Again putting the two first groups together there are 237 characters whose sum is 777282, which is considerably more than *one-half* of the whole. And again putting the first eight groups together we have 521 characters whose sum is 949074, or nearly *nine-elevenths* of the whole. On the other hand, the last or fifteenth group has (after deducting the 850 which should not be in this group) 2865 characters, which were found to occur in the whole number examined 19036 times, or less than *one-sixtieth* of the whole. And again if we add the fourteenth and fifteenth groups together we have 3410 characters, whose sum is 38533 or only about *one-thirtieth* of the whole. The character 之 *Che*, alone occurs 42068 times which is oftener than the sum total of these 3410 characters.

"From a knowledge of these facts we have been enabled to arrange a large fount of Chinese metallic type in so compact a manner that the compositor can reach any type he wants without moving more than a step in any direction; and by having placed, say five hundred, of the most numerous characters together, he has more than *three-fourths* of all he uses just under his hand, almost as conveniently as a fount of Roman type are arranged in an English printing office. The result of this arrangement has been to render the work of the compositor at least three times as rapid and cheap as it could be done under the old arrangement of the fount."

It is certain that the proportions of Mr. Gamble's list will hold good, with very little alteration, for the entire range of classical Chinese, all the works examined, having been revised by native writers on classic models; though they would undergo considerable modification, if applied to the Mandarin or other vernacular dialects. They not only confirm the observation of that early Sinologue Premare, that "a good knowledge of four or five thousand characters is sufficient for all ordinary purposes," but furnish us with a safe guide in *selecting* that limited number.

A word as to the form, in which these characters are marshalled.

Solon published his laws in verse; and for the same reason a judicious mother makes rhyme the vehicle of her nursery lessons. We thus remember the length of the months, long lines of kings, and many detached facts, which might long since have been given to the winds, but for the jingling chain that binds them together. Two senseless syllables imprint on the brain the colors of the solar spectrum; and longer, but equally senseless words serve to fix in memory the classifications of Grammar and the formulas of Logic. How much more powerful the association, when sense, sound and rythm are all combined! We have then a "three-fold cord not easily broken". With such a bond I have sought to connect these pearls, collected as it were from the ocean sands.

The credit of executing the plan is due, in no small degree, to my Chinese scribe, *Ho Sien-sheng*, a Bachelor of Nankin; and whatever defects attach to mine, I am sure, competent judges will agree that he has performed his part with exquisite skill.

He was placed under more embarrassing restrictions than those imposed on themselves by the monkish triflers of the middle ages, or our own acrostic and alliterative poets of the last two centuries.

The first law of the composition, as of its native model, the 千字文 *Ts'ien ts wen*, was that each word should occur but once.

The second, that he should confine himself to two thousand characters previously collected.

The third, that this limited number was to be subdivided into parcels of a few hundreds each, beyond which he was not at liberty to expatiate.

With all these disadvantages to contend against, in addition to the restraints of verse, *Ho Sien-sheng* has succeeded in producing a *poem*, the first half of which is almost as lucid and free, as it could have been, if the treasures of the Lexicon had been placed at his disposal. The latter part, from the nature of the case, is a little more obscure, but it reflects no less credit on the ingenuity of the composer.

The author of the *Ts'ien ts wen*, if tradition is to be believed, might have adopted the language of the Prisoner of Chillon.

> "My hair is grey; but not with years,
> Nor grew it white
> In a single night
> As men's have grown from sudden fears".

They "grew white in a single night", but it was in consequence of the exertion required in arranging in a poetical form, a thousand arbitrary words—a task imposed on him by a despotic master. Ho and I, who only *fungor vice cotis*, may not exhibit the same outward demonstration of our labors; but we have experienced enough to believe the story of our predecessor in the thorny path.*

II. *The Analysis of Characters.*

The object of this part is to introduce the foreign learner to the orthography of the language, and to supply the Chinese with what they have never had—a *Spelling Book.*

The want of that elementary manual, may excite Surprise, but the reason is obvious. Their language, is not, as ours, essentially phonetic; and the analysis of its sounds affords no clue to the composition of its characters. With us orthoepy and orthography are intimately connected, and mutually aid each other, though they are far from coinciding. In China, they altogether part company; one speaks wholly to the ear, the other addresses itself entirely to the eye. The system of *fan ts'ih* 反切 relates to the former; the latter, which is incomparably more difficult, has to be learned without the aid of any system. The dictionary presents each character as a whole, and sometimes gives its component parts by way of conjecture as to its origin. But a simple manual, which proceeds from the parts to the whole, presenting first the elements, and then the words resulting from their combination, is still a desideratum.

There is proof too, that the want has been felt; at least in one small class of words: and in the same contracted corner, an expedient has sprung up which is worthy of being employed on a more extended scale. Custom requires the Chinese, on meeting to ask each other for their family names; but many of them being similar in sound, as among ourselves, Lee, Lea, Mc.Lean, Mc.Lain, Mac.Lane, &c. it was found difficult to understand the answers without some further description. Thus:

Q. What is the name of your illustrious family?

Ans. The name of my ignoble line is *Chang*.

Q. How is it written?

Ans. It is *Stand up early chang*, not *long bow chang*; *i. e.* it is the *chang* composed of 立 and 早 not that composed of 弓 and 長: it is 章 not 張.

* A native author thus relates the origin of that curious work.

太平廣記云梁武帝於大王書中揚一千字
不重者每字片紙雜碎無序召周興嗣謂之
曰卿有才思為我韻之興嗣一夕編綴進上
鬢髮皆白

ANALYTICAL READER

The *Chings* and *Changs* are by this means distinguished into numerous clans, each wearing its own livery.

The following is a table of the surnames, which are thus familiarly analyzed.

FAMILY NAMES ANALYZED.

姓	氏	俗	解
可 人	何	月 古	胡
長 弓	張	系 子	孫
東 耳	陳	馬 二	馮
早 立	章	王 水	汪
午 言	許	古 圈	周
未 人	余	專 人	傅
肖 走	趙	衣 求	裵
子 木	李	貝 西	賈
里 立	童	呈 禾	程
包 魚	鮑	日 魚	魯
昜 木	楊	共 由	黃
工 水	江	木 雙	林
曷 艸	葛	甚 言	諶
皿 成	盛	眞 心	愼
兒 人	倪	撒 未	朱
木 八	米	欠 區	歐
者 言	諸	土 木	杜

ANALYSIS OF CHARACTERS

享	耳	郭	帅	祭		蔡
門	耳	聞	木	每		梅
丘	山	岳	龍	共		龔
口	天	吳	曲	日		曹
卯	金	劉	方	人	也	施
八	王	姜	言	身	寸	謝

This is *Spelling*; and if *names* are thus spelled out, in order to enable the hearer to write them properly, why may not other characters be subjected to the same treatment? The majority are capable of a neat division into two or three elements, each of which is a distinct whole having its own sound and sense. In this case there can hardly be a doubt as to the advantage of applying the solvent.

But there are cases in which its expediency is less clear. Where an element is neither an integer nor a radical, I have sometimes thought it worthy of separate attention, on account of its frequent occurrence in other combinations. And again where these imperfect elements closely resemble certain characters; as the parts of 民 differ but slightly from 口 *Ke'u* and 氏 *Shü*, I have thought it safe to borrow the names of those characters for the sake of preserving the recollection of that resemblance, leaving the difference to be learned by observation. It is better to run the risk of learning them with a trifling error than not to learn them at all. So the natives have thought, who give 耳東 as the components of 陳, and 口天 as those of 吳.

I may as well remark here, that the whole design of this little manual is to aid the student in getting the characters as they are now written; not to serve him as a guide to their etymology. For that, he must penetrate deeper than the forms of the living present, exhume fossils, pursue them through successive ages, and divers metamorphoses; and then become acquainted, not with families, as in the languages of western Asia, but with individuals, an employment certainly not the most edifying for a beginner. Our analysis will familiarize him with the composition of characters; but it will be for the vulgar end of enabling him to read and write, not the gratification of philological curiosity. It agrees in the main, with the distinction of radicals and primitives; but it does not proceed on it as a basis, because that would be fatal to the end in view, which be it remembered, is *orthography*—not etymology. This compels us to place the upper element before the lower, and the left before the right, irrespective of the position of the radical, *because this is the order which the natives observe in writing.*

To begin with the radical, would be like spelling an English word by beginning with the root or suffix. Again, in dissecting characters with this view, it is of less moment to hit the joints than to divide them in such a manner that they may readily be recomposed. It is easier to spell *cy-clops*, than *cycl-ops*.

III. *The Translation.*

A translation injurious to a lad, may be highly beneficial to a person of mature judgment. It is for such only, that the present is made; and for so terse a composition, something of the kind is not merely a convenience, but a necessity. The style is exceedingly elliptical, and with all the aid of native teachers, and dictionaries, the learner would be liable to lose the meaning of many a sentence. This translation, though not superseding those indispensable auxiliaries, is so constructed, as in a degree, to perform the office of both.

The mode of rendering is determined by the end proposed. If that were to introduce the reader, to a Chinese poem, I should choose those expressions best suited to represent its thoughts and spirit. But the end is the study of words; and this obliges me *reddere verbum verbo.*

As far as the sense would admit, I have given only the fundamental significations, leaving the reader to infer those that are collateral and derivative. For instance, 生 is rendered *life;* and this places him in possession of its other meanings, such as *live, alive,* to *beget, bear, be born* &c. Each character, in general, may thus play several parts—appearing without any change of form, as a substantive, adjective, verb, or adverb, according to its position in a sentence—a feature of the language, which makes the knowledge of two thousand an important acquisition.

Words introduced to complete the sense, excepting particles and pronouns, are printed in italics.

The *order* of the text has been strictly adhered to, and each line represented by a verse in the translation; so that the reader can easily ascertain what words and characters correspond—an arrangement which renders it equally available for a student of either language.

This rule, which in any language would be fatal to the elegance of a translation, is peculiarly embarassing in Chinese; and while endeavoring to make it strictly literal it has sometimes been necessary to neglect a grammatical idiom in order to give due relief to the idea of each particular character.

IV. *The mode of study.*

The student may learn the characters from the simple text by the help of the translation, and the elements from the table in Part III. marking opposite to each its sound as given by a Chinese teacher according to the dialect which he desires to cultivate. When the first chapter is completed, some book, say the christain 三字經 which is much easier than the native work of the same name, or one of the Gospels, may be taken up by way of practice. The student will be surprised to find himself already in possession of more than one half of the characters. On completing the second chapter, he would have more than nine tenths, and on arriving at the end of the fourth chapter, he will make the pleasing discovery that in any ordinary book the unknown characters are few.

The reading of native tracts on moral subjects* will then prove an agreeable pastime; and the Confucian Classics, with this preparation, will be found less arduous than they are usually regarded.

In order to acquire a thorough mastery of these staple characters, it would be well for the student to proceed to Part III, and apply himself to their orthography. For this purpose he should prepare a blank book ruled in columns answering to the vertical lines of the Chinese. In this the sounds and sense of the characters, and their elements should be written down; placing the elements first. Thus:—

    Yih | Muh | We
    One | Wood | Not-yet &c.

One or two lines might be taken as a lesson; the sounds committed to memory precisely as a column in an English spelling book; and the characters recomposed by combining the elements.

---

* The following are some of the most elegant and popular.

朱子家訓 *Chu-ts' Family Monitor.*
關帝覺世經 *Kwan-ti's Classic for Wakening the World.*
文昌陰騭文 *Wen-chang's Essay on Providence.*
太上感應篇 *T'ai-shang's tract on Retribution.*
戒溺女文 *A Dissuasive Essay on the Drowning of Daughters.*

It should not be regarded as learned until all the characters can be reproduced from the written sounds, without reference to the printed text. To aid in fixing these select characters in the mind, at once and forever, a kind of mnemonics will be found of great service. The student should invent them for himself; seizing on any association, however absurd, which may happen to strike his fancy. The following may serve as specimens.

MNEMONICS.

惟	心 隹	The ONLY needful—an *excellent heart*.
大	一 人	GREAT—*one-man*, the Emperor.
天	一 大	HEAVEN—the *one great*.
地	土 也	The EARTH is *earth*.
池	水 也	A POND is *water*.
海	水 每	The SEA—*water everywhere*.
秋	火 禾	AUTUMN—*fire* in the *rice* fields.
善	羊 口	GOOD—a *lamb*-like *mouth*.
惡	亞 心	EVIL—an *inferior heart*.
禁	林 示	PROHIBITION—*showing* two *trees* and forbidding one.
性	心 生	NATURE—the *heart born* with us.
煙	火 西 土	SMOKE (of opium)—the *fire* of the *western dirt*.
獄	犭 言 犬	A LAWSUIT—*words* between two *dogs*.
聖	耳 口 王	The SAGE—a *prince* with *ear* and *mouth* i. e. a great teacher.

The Chinese see in 爲 a resemblance to 馬 and describe it as 馬 爲 *ma we*; why may not we, in 來 to COME, see 从 人 十 *three men coming to a cross road?* In 從 to FOLLOW, see 从 卜 *five men following* an augur &c.?

Associations arbitrary and ludicrous are sanctioned by native usage; and the foreign student would do well not to despise them.

When the two thousand characters are thoroughly mastered, it will be of great advantage to go over them, writing under each such others as may be connected with it, by regular derivation, or casual resemblance. Thus:

未 Suggests 木 末 本 昧 抹 妹 &c.
生 ------- 性 姓 星 醒 腥 笙 產 &c.
民 ------- 氏 氓 泯 &c.
來 ------- 徠 棶 饕 &c.

前 ------- 箭 剪 翦 &c.
有 ------- 宥 囿 賄 &c.
上 ------- 止 正 旨 &c.
帝 ------- 締 締 蹄 &c.

The habit of thus grouping on a familiar basis, all the characters, the student may be able to recall, will augment the amount of his treasures, and confirm him in their possession. In this manner, the original number may easily be tripled or quadrupled.

An appropriate sequel to the study of these common characters, will be that of the several styles in which they are written. These are six in number.

1. 宋書 The clear square letter usually preferred in books, and so called from the dynasty of Sung, under which it came in vogue in connexion with the art of printing, then first invented.

2. 楷書 The Pattern style—the happy mean between the stiff sharp angles of the foregoing, and the wavy, flowing, but uncertain lines of the two following. The most important documents are always engrossed in *Kiai-shu*; and large works are frequently printed in it.

3. 行書 Running-hand—that employed in ordinary business.

4. 草書 The grass letter—running hand run wild, so as to resemble entangled grass. Though courtesy requires the scholar to apply the name of *ts'au ts* as a depreciative epithet to any specimen of his own chirography; to attain grace and ease in the management of this style is an object of ambition.

5. 隸書 an ornamental hand formerly employed in engrossing official documents, whence the name; though for that purpose, it has now given place to the *Kiai-shu*. It is still much used however, for scrolls, monumental inscriptions, and book-prefaces.

6. 篆書 by foreigners called the Seal character on account of its most frequent use. It is also much used for inscriptions on monuments and in adorning the title pages of books.

The 1st. 2nd. and 5th. stand related to each other somewhat as the Roman, Italic, and Black-letter of our letter press.

The 3rd., 4th., and 6th., may be compared to the Round hand, Running hand, and German text of our chirography. But while, in our own printing and penmanship; all the varieties may be learned, by a little attention to the comparison of a few forms; to acquire a knowledge of the different styles in Chinese, is a labor of more difficulty. It requires the careful comparison of of some hundreds of leading forms, and in addition to this, the aid of constant practice.

But this is a task which the student will hardly feel himself at liberty to decline. For without it, he is liable to be confounded, not merely confused, by constantly meeting his old friends in new disguises. Not only will he be perplexed by inscriptions on monuments, which he meets in travelling, and the prefaces or title-pages of elegant works; but the proclamation of a mandarin, the bill of a shop-keeper, or the letter of a native friend, will prove an annoying puzzle. The foreign student of German may indulge his tastes, without troubling himself to decipher reams of *handschrift*; but if resident on the banks of the Rhine he would find it somewhat inconvenient not to be able to learn for himself the contents of a familiar note. For the resident in China, the styles of business and correspondence are equally indispensable.

The six styles are arranged in the order of their importance. The first is that used in the text and analysis; and the reader will have the advantage of seeing it in at least two sizes of type.

Of the others, specimens and exercises are included in Part III. and for materials to practice on, the learner needs be at no loss. Monuments, sign-boards, prefaces, and letters— old ones which a native friend may submit to his perusal—will all come to his aid and further his progress.

VI. *Use in Schools.*

With us the first stages in climbing the hill of knowledge are so gentle that the young scholar saunters on unconscious of effort. In China they are so precipitous, that a large proportion of those who attempt the ascent, fall back in despair. To grade the steep, facilitate the acquisition of the elements of education, and promote the efficiency of christian schools was my prime object in preparing the Chinese portion of this work.

Via trita via tuta is a good maxim; but it should not prevent us mending the "old paths". That they have been trodden by the feet of millions is no evidence that they are incapable of improvement. Foreigners in China have not felt compelled to use wooden blocks in printing their books, just because the Chinese have done so ever since the invention of printing. And if metallic types and revolving presses are improvements on the native mode of manufacturing books, why should it be taken as a foregone conclusion that the foreigner can suggest no better method for acquiring a knowledge of their contents?

Is it not a fact that the majority of pupils in Chinese schools, never succeed in learning to read and write? And is it not an equally significant fact, that the man who can read fluently, and write correctly is regarded as a scholar? The apparatus for obtaining knowledge passes for learning, and rudiments are esteemed accomplishments.

To a certain extent this is owing to the difficulty of the written language, which is not much easier for the native, than it is for the foreign student; but it is due in part to imperfections in the method of teaching.

A boy of eight summers attired for the occasion, in robes of ceremony, selecting a lucky day, enters on the career of a scholar, by doing obeisance to his teacher, and kneeling before the picture of Confucius. A book is placed in his hands, and he is taught the *sounds* of some half a dozen characters. These learned, he hands the book to the teacher, and turning his back recites his lesson in a sing-song tone, keeping time like a pendulum by the vibrations of his body. Day after day, he goes on cramming his memory with sounds and forms until he can patter off the Four Books and the Book of Odes as glibly as a breviary. But all this time he has not obtained the glimmering of an idea. He has got the symbols of thought, but not the thoughts.

This ordeal passed, he is deemed worthy of initiation into higher mysteries. The veil is gradually withdrawn, and a ray of light shed on each of those dull figures, kindling them into life, and transforming empty sounds into the articulate voices of human language.

The intellect of the lad feels the stimulus, and wakes as from a hibernation; while his faculties unfold like the buds of Spring. Reading becomes a pleasure; and he delights to employ those signs—not till now 'significant—for the expression of his own thoughts.

But how many youth are compelled by poverty to quit school before the dawn of this cheering period! And how many more toil on for years in unalleviated darkness because they are too dull to complete the preliminary process to the satisfaction of their teachers! What would be thought of the school-master who should compel his pupils to commit the Iliad to memory before translating a line? Yet this is precisely the time-honored system of the Chinese; and it is doing it no wrong to charge it with perpetrating the crime of mental infanticide on an enormous scale.

A partial remedy applied in many mission schools, is to require the teacher to deviate so far from the beaten track as to connect the sense of each character with its form and sound in the very commencement of his instructions. A further melioration would be to furnish the student with a selection of those characters in most common use, as the readiest way to the treasures of knowledge; and to teach him from the first to *spell* each one as an aid to memory, and a preparation for writing.

How far the first of these conditions will be met by the following collection may be inferred from the account already given of the principles on which it is formed, and whether the second will be answered by the analytical method, may also be inferred from the explantion on a previous page. It only remains therefore, to add an observation or two in regard to the mode of teaching.

Who of us does not remember the young emulation which impelled us to learn pages of words, before we had any appreciation of their value, merely from the hope of standing at the head of a spelling-class? How intense the feeling grew when the school was divided into parties, and the combatants entered the lists two and two; the victorious boy, wearing his honors as proudly as a champion of the ring!

The Chinese system of education is not destitute of this stimulus. The more advanced students contend for academic and civil honors with an ardor unsurpassed in any country. But it is wanting at that stage, at which an incentive is most needed. In the early portion of his course, each pupil pursues a solitary path, receives instruction alone, and recites alone, knowing little and caring less as to the progress of his fellows. In most primary schools, the class organization is wholly unknown, and the teacher repeats for each individual an amount of toil which would suffice for a whole form. By this mode of spelling these inconveniences may be obviated—the spur applied to the pupil, and labor saved to the teacher: classes may be formed, and recitations conducted precisely as in an English school, though in learning their lessons, pupils will require an amount of oral instruction, which is not called for in a language whose orthography is more purely phonetic.

An experiment made in our mission school while these sheets were passing through the press has proved highly satisfactory. In the morning, the teacher calls a class before him and gives them the sound and sense of the characters and their elements, and then requires them to copy the lesson into a book provided for the purpose in order to impress it on the memory, and accustom them to writing. In the afternoon he summons them to recite. He pronounces a character of the text, and the first pupil responds by giving its elements. The next character is analyzed by the second boy, and so on, until some one makes a mistake; when the character is passed on, and the boy who succeeds in spelling it correctly is promoted to the place of him who failed.

The exercise proves novel and exciting; and some of the boys who previously appeared indifferent as to progress, have begun to apply themselves with diligence. Memoriter recitation, definition of characters, translation into the Mandarin or vernacular dialect, and writing on the black-board, are additional exercises in which it is sought to inspire the pupils with the same emulation, and so render their progress pleasant as well as thorough.

I conclude this introduction with a statement of *Ching Siensheng*, a Nankin *Siu-ts'ai*, who is in charge of the school. "Since having the care of a school, I have often grieved over the difficulty experienced by young pupils in learning the points and strokes of our letters. Lately however a work has been prepared, entitled *Jin-ts-sing-fah*—"A new Method for Learning Characters". The method consists in resolving one character into several, and combining several into one. The most frequent characters in the Four Books and Five Classics are thus elucidated, so that the student not only learns them with little trouble, but gets at the ideas which gave birth to the characters. Moreover in learning one, he obtains a knowledge of three. I have employed this method in the instruction of my pupils and found it both expeditious and thorough". *

. *. Part III. is published in a separate form for the use of schools.

PART II.

THE TEXT AND TRANSLATION.

常字雙千

CONSTANT CHARACTERS, A COUPLE OF THOUSANDS,

Note. .

Chap I. Contains 237 characters which occur, from 1000, to 10000 times, in the books examined, and the three following from the next group. 羣溫昭

Chap II. Contains 587 characters which occur from 200 to 1000 times, with the addition of the five following from the next groups. 欺邀僑恭讓

Chap III. Contains 570 characters, which occur from 75 to 200 times, and six additional from the next groups. 稽均雒袍綻珍

Chap IV. Contains the the most frequent characters in the remaining groups, with an intermixture of useful characters compiled from other sources—in all 608. See page 4.

The sum total of the four chapters is 2016.

The sounds are given according to the current Mandarin.

The vowels are those of the German, except that *i* and *e* before *n* and *ng* have the force of *i* in *fin*, and *ŭ* in *fun*, *s*, *ts*, *ch*, and *sh* standing alone, have a strong sibillation, as in *rats*, *church*, *pass*, *hush* when the **sound** is prolonged.

The Greek aspirate represents a breathing, which can only be learned from the living teacher.

第一章論古始 (ti yih chang len ku sh)

造物 (we sheng ming lai)

1. 未生民來　前有上帝　惟一眞神　無聖能比
   (we sheng ming lai / ts'ien yiu shang ti / we yih chen shin / wu sheng neng pi)

2. 六日力作　先闢天地　萬物多焉　既希且異
   (luh jih lih tsuh / sien p'ih t'ien ti / wan wuh to yien / ki hi ts'ia i)

3. 遂亦和土　將爲靈矣　命處賜基　千百皆與
   (sue yih ho t'u / tsiang we ling i / ming ch'u ts'ki / ts'ien pah kiai yü)

4. 復使宜家　女兮徃事　謂之曰夫　爾我如自
   (fuh sh i kia / nü hi wang sh / we ch yuih fu / r wo ju ts)

CHAPTER. I.

DISCOURSES OF THE ANCIENT BEGINNINGS.

Creation

1.
Not-yet to life *were* people come,
Before existed the Supreme Ruler,
Only One True God,
No holy *one* can compare *with him*.

2.
Six days *he* mightily wrought,
First divided Heaven and Earth,
Myriads of things multiplied (0),*a*
Both rare AND strange.

3.
Then also tempered clay,
Intending to make a spiritual being,
Decreed *his* place in the bestowed possession,
By thousands and hundreds all *things* gave.

4.
Again *he* sent *one* to order the family,
Woman (0) went to serve *him*,
And calling him, said, "Husband,
Thou and I *are* as *one* self".

墮惡

5. 凡(fan) 所(so) 求(k'iu) 者(che)
毋(wu) 不(puh) 立(lih) 予(yü)
然(jan) 欲(yuh) 善(shan) 惡(oh)
勿(wuh) 聽(t'ing) 手(sheu) 取(k'ü)

6. 告(kau) 云(yuin) 可(k'o) 食(shih)
或(hwoh) 當(tang) 見(kien) 耳(r)
聞(wen) 言(yien) 摩(mo) 拿(na)
得(tah) 罪(tsue) 因(yin) 此(ts')

7. 中(chung) 傳(chuan) 亞(ya) 伯(peh)
羊(yang) 祭(tsi) 信(sing) 心(sin)
長(chang) 子(ts) 若(joh) 見(hiung)
敵(tih) 殺(shah) 及(kih) 今(king)

8. 以(i) 致(ch) 彼(pe) 族(ts'uh)
但(tan) 安(an) 利(li) 名(ming)
愛(ai) 身(shin) 尼(niih) 色(sah)
列(lih) 馬(ma) 羅(lo) 金(king)

9. 爻(fu) 意(i) 非(fe) 昔(sih)
其(k'i) 僕(p'oh) 巳(i) 明(ming)
卽(tsih) 由(yiu) 是(sh) 時(sh)
大(ta) 水(shue) 四(s) 行(hing)

The Fall.

5.
Of all which *they* desired (0),
There was nothing not instantly granted,
Yet wished *they* the good and evil *fruit*,
They must-not listen to the hand's taking *it*.

6.
One informed *them* saying "Can eat,
Perhaps *you* ought to see". (0),
They heard the words, felt and took,
Getting sin *was* because-of this.

7.
Their second son *b* Abel *c* (2)
Sheep offered, with a believing heart,
Their elder (longer) son, as elder-brother,
Vengefully killed *him; thus it is* till now.

8.
So caused that race,
Solely to rest in gain and name,
To love the body and dote-on beauty,
Multiply horses and gather gold.

9.
The Father's mind was-not as formerly,
His servant already clearly-*saw*,
Then from that time,
The great waters to the four *quarters* went.

10		11		12		13		14	
卷	küin	居	kü	隆救		等	teng	相	siang
撒	sah	八	pah	故	ku	間	kien	約	yoh
全	ts'üin	從	ts'ung	又	yiu	于	yü	眾	chung
死	s	七	ts'ih	督	toh	三	sau	士	s
				教	kiau				
何	ho	各	koh	甚	sheng	倫	len	必	pih
問	wen	拉	la	加	kia	出	ch'uh	知	ch
儕	ch'ai	入	juh	世	sh	於	yü	理	li
羣	k'üin	門	men	福	fuh	五	wu	數	su
第	ti			降	kiang	華	hwa	節	tsih
歸	kwe			下	hia	年	nien	禮	li
方	fang			耶	ye	至	ch	守	sheu
蓋	kai			穌	su	殿	tien	法	fah
則	tsah			斯	s	在	tsai	司	s
同	t'ung			實	shih	會	hwe	十	shih
義	i			救	kiu	受	sheu	二	r
人	jin			主	chu	書	shu	徒	t'u

10.
Whirled, scattered, the whole *world* died—
Why ask for classes and companies!
But *those who* turned to the square shelter,
Then *were* the same-with righteous men.

11.
The dwellers eight, their followers
      (the animals) were by sevens,
Each drew *them* into the gate.

Redemption.

12.
Therefore again, *He* watched-over taught,
And greatly adding to the world's happiness,
Sent down Jesus, (2)
He *is* really the Saving Lord.

13.
In rank, the midst OF Three,
In relations *he* came-out OF the Five,[a]
In the flower of *his* years, came-to the temple,
In the assembly,[c] *he* received the books.

14.
He joined in covenant many scholars,
Certainly understood principles and numbers,
Regulated rites, observed laws,
And controlled *his* twelve disciples.

15

冷 len
迦 kia
城 ch'eng
邑 yih

巴 pa
米 mi
道 tau
路 lu

猶 yiu
太 t'ai
國 kwoh
也 ye

西 si
乃 nai
山 shan
乎 hu

16

王 wang
而 r
溫 wen
雅 ya

後 heu
章 chang
昭 chau
諸 chu

凡二百四十字

15.

Jerusalem and Capernaum, a city and town,
To Babylon and Media *were* ways and roads,
Judea (2) *was* a kingdom (0),
Sinai (0) a mountain (0).

16.

A King, yet (and) meek and gentle,
The after chapter illustrates these.

Notes.

a. (0) Marks the place of an expletive, which is untranslatable.
   (2) indicates that two characters are rendered by one word.
   ( ) indicates that the word enclosed is the usual rendering, or an obvious explanation.
b. Lit. middle propagation.
c. In Foreign names, the characters stand only for syllables. Those for Abel, are 亞 *inferior* or *secondly*, and 伯 *lord* or *uncle*.
d. The 五倫 five social relations. 君臣, 父子, 夫婦, 兄弟, 朋友. The "flower of his years"—at the age of twelve.
e. The Synagogue. Luke IV. 16.
f. In names, the first or last character is frequently taken for the whole. The following are the significations of those in this verse 冷 *cold,* 迦 a *Budhist deity,* 巴 *a handful, gripe or blow,* 米 *rice,* 猶 *like, yet,* 太 *great, huge,* 西 *west,* 乃 (0).

ANALYTICAL READER.

第二章論耶穌興教
ti r chang lūn ye su hing kiau

綱領
ts'ing ying

1 親營皮幕
ts'ing ying p'i mo

赦過拯逃
sheh ko ch'eng t'au

蒙選代贖
mung süen tai shuh

聲稱益高
sheng ch'eng yih kau

2 備歷苦難
pe lih k'u nan

顯成功勞
hien ch'eng kung lau

追厥本初
chue küih pen ts'u

垂訓汝曹
chu'e hüing ju ts'au

出世
3 母氏瑟妻
mu sh sah ts'i

少小待字
shau siau tai ts

蓮容素端
lien yung su tuan

蘭性較細
lan sing kiau si

4 曾緣夢感
ts'en yuen mung kan

忽產男嗣
hwoh ch'an nan s

CHAPTER II.

TREATS OF THE RISE OF CHRISTIANITY,

Leading Topics.

1.
Himself *a* formed a skin tabernacle,
Pardoned transgression, succored refugees,
In the chosen's (2) stead *paid* ransom—
His fame and praise *become* more high.

2.
He fully passed-through bitter hardships,
Displayed complete his meritorious toil,
Pursuing ʜɪs original beginning,
We will condescendingly instruct you (2).

Christ's Advent.

3.
His mother (2) Joseph's wife,
Of few *years* and small, waiting marriage *b*,
Was of lily face and habitually correct,
Her fragrant nature incomparably refined.

4.
Having *from* a dream conceived,
She suddenly gave-birth to a male heir.

受洗

9
向 hiang
野 ye
翰 han
呼 hu

悔 hwe
改 kai
務 wu
切 ts'ih

就 tsiu
洗 si
河 ho
旁 p'ang

循 sün
儀 i
莫 moh
越 hüih

8
畜 hioh
老 lau
革 keh
荒 hwang

龍 lung
現 hien
首 sheu
舉 kü

免 mien
歟 yü
幸 hing
哉 tsai

原 yuen
靡 mi
終 chung
始 sh

7
追 tai
君 küing
卒 tsoh
沒 moh

率 soh
眷 küen
返 fan
止 ch

仍 jin
恐 k'ung
勒 lah
召 chau

挪 no
貧 fu
脫 t'oh
去 k'ü

6
后 heu
皇 hwang
最 tsue
忍 jin

按 an
戶 hu
戮 luh
刑 hing

夜 ye
深 sheng
投 t'eu
遠 yuen

避 pi
境 king
藏 ts'ang
形 hing

嬰時

5
東 tung
界 kiai
友 yiu
師 sh

軍 küing
光 kwang
詳 ts'iang
視 sh

造 ts'au
室 shih
辱 juh
臨 ling

伏 fuh
拜 pai
依 i
炙 ts'

His Infancy.

5.

From the Eastern border, friendly Masters,
The host of lights minutely beholding,
Approach the room, humbly arrive,
Bow-down and worship according-to order.

6.

The king (2) was most unfeeling,
Each door he cruelly punished,
At night late (deep) *Joseph* dashed afar,
And flying the region hid his person.

7.

Waiting till the prince deceased (2),
He led his relations and returning stopped,
Yet afraid-of a compulsory summons,
Escaping bore away *the child* and went.

8.

When a beast is old, his hide is bare,'
When a dragon appears, his head is raised,
Escaped (avoided)(0)! *how* fortunate(0)!
Originally he *has* no end or beginning.

His Baptism.

9.

Towards the desert John cried,
Repent, reform, take-care *to be* earnest.
Christ came to baptism at the river's brink,
Observed the rite, and did not transgress.

10	11 見試	12	13	14 宣道
譬 pi	嘗 ch'ang	拼 ping	修 siu	乘 ch'eng
樹 shu	遇 yu	令 ling	德 tah	驢 lü
結 kih	魔 mo	俯 fu	圖 t'u	歡 hwan
果 ko	試 sh	望 wang	報 pau	樂 luh
適 shih	指 ch	尊 tsun	正 chen	總 tsung
口 k'eu	餅 ping	榮 yung	直 chih	集 tsih
維 we	爭 tseng	強 k'iang	兩 liang	智 ch
悅 yüih	遺 i	施 sh	虛 hü	愚 yü
否 feu	押 yah		奉 fung	條 t'iau
悉 sih	登 teng		諭 yü	誡 kiai
刃 jin	宮 kung		遵 tsun	張 chang
斷 tuan	屋 uh		遣 k'ien	布 pu
便 pien	崇 ts'ung		烏 u	宰 tsai
付 fu	垣 wan		敢 kan	治 ch
焚 fen	被 pe		惑 hoh	屬 shuh
烈 lih	擕 hi		余 yü	吾 wu

10.

He used the parable of a tree bearing fruit;
Suiting the mouth it *only* gives pleasure,
Otherwise, totally the blade will-cut *it down*,
Thereon *to be* handed-over to burning fierce.

His Temptation.

11.

He once met the Devil's trying,
Who pointing to loaves, strove to bestow them
And carrying him ascended a palatial house,
To a lofty wall WAS he led-up.

12.

Also bidding him bend-down and look *abroad*,
Exalted glory he forcibly offered (gave).

13.

"To cultivate virtue mapping-out its rewards,
Makes honesty and rectitude both void.
Obeying orders fulfilling my mission,
How dare you tempt me"!

His preaching.

14. .

He rode an ass when he rejoiced (2),
Together gathered the wise and stupid,
The lines of command, spread-out (2),
Saying "To rule and govern belongs to me.

施訓

15	16	17	18	19
攻 kung 擊 kih 違 we 逆 niih	陷 hien 謀 meu 亡 wang 獄 yuh	花 hwa 嫩 neng 易 i 敗 pai	懼 kü 失 sh 災 tsai 絕 tsüih	孰 shuh 忘 wang 足 tsuh 畏 we
常 ch'ang 聚 tsü 俊 ching 英 ing	遭 tsau 患 hwan 沙 sha 洲 cheu	麥 meh 掃 sau 定 ting 留 liu	好 hau 甲 kiah 亂 luan 俱 kü	頓 tun 害 hai 體 t'i 魂 hwon
旨 ch 斥 ch'ih 氣 k'i 責 tsah	統 t'ung 轄 hiah 的 tih 裔 i	類 lue 反 fan 鳥 niau 獸 sheu	仇 ch'eu 怒 nu 財 ts'ai 據 kü	該 kai 恃 sh 庇 pi 釋 shih
隱 ing 暗 an 畢 pih 陳 ch'eng	征 chen 途 t'u 遍 pien 周 cheu	穀 kuh. 養 yang 弗 fuh 憂 yiu	兵 ping 奪 toh 車 ch'e 驅 k'ü	藉 tsch 謝 sie 恩 en 仁 jin

15.

I attack and smite disobedient opposers,
Constantly collect the excellent and brave,
Self-will reprove, passion (vapor) rebuke,
The secret and dark, to the utmost display."

16.

He fell-into plots, and fled *d* imprisonment,
Encountered affliction in the sandy isles,*e*
Generally swayed the lineal descendants,
In progressive journeys everywhere circula-
   ted.

His Teachings.

17.

The flower *f* tender easily wastes,
Wheat in sweeping is certainly retained.
Our race *is* contrary to birds and beasts,
Which for grain to nourish do-not grieve.

18.

Dread loss, and calamity will-cease,
Love war, and confusion comes-with it,
If hatred rages, and riches are clutched,
Soldiers seize and chariots drive *them away.*

19.

Who forgets *him who is* enough to be feared?
He at-once injures body and soul.
You ought to rest-on his protection (2),
Dependently thank his grace and goodness.

	20	21 立教	22	23 定例	24
1	學 hioh / 別 pih / 派 p'ai / 支 ch	海 hai / 干 kan / 哥 ko / 弟 ti	目 muh / 紀 ki / 矜 k'ing / 恤 süih	邦 pang / 都 tu / 省 sheng / 京 king	燔 fan / 牡 meu / 割 koh / 肉 juh
2	埃 yai / 田 t'ien / 許 hü / 置 ch	棄 k'i / 業 yeh / 速 suh / 起 k'i	志 ch / 揚 yang / 讚 tsan / 美 me	南 nan / 北 peh / 半 pan / 經 king	舊 kiu / 例 li / 雖 sue / 存 ts'un
3	敬 king / 妄 wang / 良 liang / 分 fen	履 li / 武 wu / 請 ts'ing / 隨 sue	犬 meh / 記 ki / 祈 k'i / 文 wen	每 me / 念 nian / 僭 tsien / 僞 we	羔 kau / 牛 niu / 特 t'ah / 犢 tuh
4	詛 tsu / 禁 king / 祝 chuh / 極 kih	願 yuen / 離 li / 鄉 hiang / 里 li	通 t'ung / 達 tah / 古 ku / 史 sh	化 hwa / 導 tau / 平 p'ing / 情 ts'ing	錫 sih / 獻 hien / 豈 k'i / 欣 hing

20.

The doctrine distinguishes classes (2),
Some in Eden (2), it promises to place,
Reverence and deceit, it well divides,
To curse forbids, in blessing *is* extreme.

His Disciples.

21.

By the sea, he called the brothers [g] (2),
They cast-aside their business, hasten to rise,
His sandal steps beg to follow,
Willing to forsake their neighborhood (2).

22.

Their eyes recorded his compassions (2),
With a will they spread his praise,
Silently memorised the prayer-form,
Opened (2) *their minds* to ancient history.

23.

Kingdom, capital, province, metropolis,
North and South, they half traversed,
Ever thinking [h] of the blasphemous and false,
Reformed, led them, calmed their passions.

His Ordinances.

24.

Burnt males and the cutting of the flesh,
By the old ordinance, though retained,
Yet lamb, cow, ox, and calf,
As gifts, and offerings, what pleasure?

29	28	27 行奇	26	25
助 tsu	詣 i	鬼 kwe	著 chu	私 s
竿 han	船 ch'uan	逐 chuh	語 yü	儞 yü
賴 lai	波 po	病 ping	貴 kwe	公 kung
他 t'a	面 mien	醫 i	喻 yü	禱 tau
審 sheng	息 sih	汚 wu	奇 k'i	葡 p'u
判 p'an	風 fung	解 kiai	畧 lioh	萄 t'au
咸 hien	舟 cheu	禍 ho	更 ken	飲 ing
已 ki	底 ti	滅 mih	接 tsih	傾 k'ing
罰 fah	愈 yü	葬 tsang	顧 ku	開 k'ai
犯 fan	疾 tsih	墓 mo	種 chung	堂 t'ang
廣 kwang	環 hwan	寢 ts'ing	牧 muh	誠 ch'eng
援 yuen	觀 kwan	興 hing	傷 shang	勸 k'üen
重 chung	活 hwoh	捫 meng	夕 sih	引 ying
權 k'üen	喪 sang	衣 i	朝 chau	證 chen
獨 tuh	侍 sh	婦 fu	歲 sue	宣 süen
任 jin	喜 hi	潔 kih	月 yüih	音 ing

25.
But private supplication, public prayer,
The grape (2), to drink and pour,
To open the hall, and sincerely exhort,
Adduce evidence, and proclaim the sound:—

His Miracles.

26.
Publishing *Christ's* words, we value parables
His miracles briefly in-turn succeed,
He guarded the plant, shepherded the bruised
Evening and morning, for years and months;

27.
Devils expelled, sickness healed,
The unclean released, misery extinguished,
The buried in the grave, from slumber rose,
Touching his clothes, a woman was cleansed.

28.
He visited a boat, on the wave's face
And stilled the wind, in the bark's bottom,
Recovered sick, around looked-on *him*,
Revived dead, standing-by rejoiced.

29.
For help little *did he* depend-on another,
Even the judgment (2) is all his own,
He punishes offenders, widely rescues,
And weighty authority alone sustains.

30	31 預言	32	33 臨終	34
固 ku	散 san	廢 fe	工 kung	動 tung
保 pau	編 pien	園 yuen	役 yuh	偕 hiai
盛 sheng	賽 sai	吉 kih	貧 p'ing	新 sing
盈 ying	說 shoh	壤 jang	富 fu	娶 k'ü
恒 heng	錄 luh	頌 tsung	左 tso	香 hiang
懷 hwai	久 kiu	對 tue	右 yiu	供 kung
恭 kung	兆 chau	誰 sue	近 king	酒 tsiu
順 shun	伊 i	欺 k'i	交 kiau	邀 yau
外 wai	毀 hwe	街 kiai	餘 yü	執 tsih
暴 pau	宇 yü	歌 ko	論 lün	油 yiu
內 nue	再 tsai	谷 kuh	尤 yiu	膏 kau
慾 k'ien	建 kien	應 ing	服 fuh	坐 tso
庶 shu	預 yü	俾 pe	班 pan	流 liu
幾 ki	計 ki	讓 jang	旅 lü	血 hüih
戰 chan	末 moh	九 kiu	盡 tsing	憫 ming
勝 sheng	期 k'i	思 s	招 chau	號 hau

30.
Firmly guard abundance full,
Ever cherish respectful obedience,
And outward violence, inward depravity,
You almost-certainly (2) fight victoriously.

Prophecies.

31.
In scattered essays, Isaiah spoke,
And the record long fore-tokened IT,
The demolished temple *should* again be-built,
He fore-reckoned (2) the final period.

32.
Waste gardens turn to happy ground,
Compare (2) *the fulfilment*-who *will* despise?
In the streets songs, in the vallies answers,
Must yield to repeated[j] thought.

His Last Days

33.
Artisans, officials, poor and rich,
Left and right held near intercourse,
To his casual discourses heartily submitted,
Their class companions all summoned,

34.
Moved together-with the Bridegroom (2),
Odours offered, to wine invited,
Held oil and anointed him sitting *at meat*.
When flowed his blood, he pitiously cried.

凡五百七十六字

38	37	36	35 勸世
偶像阿回 eu siang o hwe	宗姓單徵 tsung sing tan we	察貨度銀 ts'ah ho toh yin	慧爾慈雲 hwe yü ts' yüing
銅鐵石木 t'ung t'ih sh muh	祖孫答述 tsu sun tah shuh	赤白用給 ch'ih peh yung keh	震角播示 ching koh po sh
創識破淫 ch'uang sh p'o ying	共獲濟進 kung hoh tsi tsing	提要發綱 t'i yau fah kang	背架築壇 pe kia chuh t'an
尚議變俗 shang i pien suh	誓之哀哭 sh fah ai k'uh	合享永位 hoh hiang yung we	納匱載器 nah kwe tsai k'i

Exhortation.

35.
Wisdom as the rain, mercy as the clouds,
With thundering horn disseminate, show forth
He bore the cross, *and of it* built an altar,
As priests took the ark*, and bore the vessels.

36.
Inspect the goods, estimate the silver,
The red and white*, you must give—
We have handled important, taken-up lead-
  ing-topics—
He is fit to enjoy an ever-lasting throne.

37.
His family (2), solitary and insignificant,
Grandfather, grandson answer the record—
May we together obtain conveyance to enter,
Where it-is-sworn *is* no sorrow or weeping.

38.
Image likenesses, *why* dote-on (2), ?
Brass, iron, stone, and wood,
Begin *to be* intelligent burst adulterous wiles,
Uppermost consider a change of customs.

NOTES.

a. 親 usually signifies a near relation but the usage in this place, which is a frequent one, suggests the idea that one's nearest relation is *himself*.

Hereafter the pronouns will not be italicised, where they are plainly implied. This first line contains a natural, though inelegant figure for the incarnation.

b. Lit. *letters,* referring to the marriage *contract*.

c. The disclosure of Herod's real character. The "dragon" an emblem of the divine, refers to Christ.

d. 亡 usually means to *perish*.

e. "Sandy isles"—oases.

f. Though the following lines are not exact citations of Scripture, the reader will readily recall passages in which the ideas occur.

g. Lit. *Elder brother* and *Younger brother*.

h. "Thinking" compassionately.

i. Contract for 福音 the Happy Sound, the Gospel.
There is here an ellipsis, which is readily supplied.

j. Lit. *nine thoughts*.

k. Lit. *Desk.* In. S. S. 約匱 ark of the covenant.

l. "Red and white" *Gold* and *Silver*.

CHAPTER III.

第三章論人事
ti san chang lun jin sh

4
兒輩謳誦　r pe eu tsung
賦擇詩稽　fu tsah sh ki
齒牙申講　ch' ya sheng kiang
返邇均推　hia r küing t'ñe

3　勤學
量才託授　liang ts'ai t'oh sheu
衞翼扶持　we yih fu ch'
詔戒誘誨　chau kiai yiu hwe
晝晚鑑茲　cheu wan kien ts

2
辜咎疑輕　ku kiu i k'ing
雪寃艱巨　süih yüen kien kü
覺昧醒迷　küoh me sing mi
陰府抵拒　ing fu ti kü

1　待鞠　萬事
啓穴屍甦　k'i hüih sh su
凌空升昇　ling k'ung sheng kü
寶座式憑　pau tso sh p'ing
訟詞追具　tsung ts' p'ch kü

CHAPTER III.

HUMAN AFFAIRS

Accountability.

1.
Opening the cave, his corpse revived,
Spurned the empty *air*, and rose aloft,
The jewelled throne, he rested-on (2),
Trial words, he will-speedily complete.

2.
Offences and faults, he judges[a] lightly,
Redresses[b] wrongs difficult and huge,
Arouses the blinded, awakes the deluded,
And the gloomy palace[c] withstands (2),

Diligence.

3.
Measuring talents, he commits (2), *trusts*;
Encompasses with wings, supports, holds *us*,
With edicts, prohibitions persuades instructs,
Morning and evening mirror yourself in these.

4.
The boy's class should-read and recite,
Songs select, poems search,
Front-teeth and molars, repeat, expound,
Remote and near equally generalize[d].

ANALYTICAL READER — 47

5 幼年	6	7 壯歲	8	9 士業
孩 yüen 監 kien 嬰 ing 孩 hai	秉 ping 質 chih 清 ts'ing 聰 ts'ung	幼 yiu 丁 ting 漸 tsien 壯 chuang	克 k'ah 伐 fah 驕 kiau 縱 tsung	博 poh 嗜 sh 簡 kien 篇 p'ien
胎 t'ai 元 yüen 誕 tan 育 yuh	概 kai 除 ch'u 雜 tsah 慾 yuh	習 sih 染 jan 殊 ch'u 童 t'ung	窮 kiung 抑 ih 困 kw'eng 窘 k'iung	几 ki 筵 yien 勤 k'ing 讀 t'uh
急 kih 乳 ju 泣 k'ih 饑 ki	夙 suh 謹 k'ien 洪 hung 沾 chan	詭 kwe 謙 k'ien 襲 sih 貌 mau	倘 t'ang 憾 han 墮 to 落 luh	琴 k'ing 劍 kien 逞 t'uan 遊 yiu
席 sih 臥 wo 綿 mien 束 shuh	盍 hoh 早 tsau 濯 choh 沐 muh	骸 hie 笑 siau 匪 niih 衷 chung	機 ki 術 shuh 奚 hi 庸 yung	專 ch'uan 侮 wu 愼 sheng 篤 tuh

5.
Do-but contemplate infant children,
From the womb at-first born and nourished,
Impatient for milk, they weep for hunger,
On matting sleep, in cotton wrapped.

6.
Endowed with talents[e] pure and intelligent,
Altogether exclude mixed desires,
With the primitive offence greatly tainted,
Why-not early wash (2) (foot and head)?

Youth.

7.
Tender youth gradually strengthening,
Acquire stains diverse-from lads.
Deceit and modesty lurk in the countenance,
Terror and laughter hide in the bosom,

Manhood.

8.
Emulation, and pride, *are* let-loose,
To persecute and oppress the helpless poor,
If you abhor falling[f] (2),
The instrument and art, how simple!

Scholars.

9.
Learnedly voracious of brief essays,
On bench, at feast, *some* diligently read,
Some with harp and sabre restlessly rove,
Intent on insulting the careful and solid.

49 ANALYTICAL READER

	10		11 農田		12		13 工匠		14
尸	sh	泥	ni	郊	kiau	操	ts'au	酬	ch'eu
爵	tsioh	塗	t'u	場	ch'ang	尺	ch'ih	值	chih
曠	kw'ang	奔	peng	收	sheu	運	yüng	竭	kih
官	kwan	走	tseu	積	tsih	斤	king	償	ch'ang
貪	t'an	竊	ts'ih	繼	ki	係	hi	泉	ts'üen
祜	hu	認	jin	蹟	tsih	誇	kw'a	刀	tau
祀	s	農	nung	厚	heu	傑	kih	還	hwan
佛	fuh	耕	keng	豐	fung	步	pu	互	hu
哄	fah	澤	tsah	疇	ch'eu	弓	kung	苟	keu
唎	li	灌	kwan	想	siang	矢	sh	悟	wu
嚨	sai	烟	yien	寅	ying	皿	ming	了	liau
朋	p'ung	植	chih	鞠	küih	料	liau	休	hiu
輪	lun	抹	moh	曲	k'üih	精	tsing	連	lin
須	sü	露	lu	跪	kwe	粗	ts'u	番	fan
鑒	kien	踐	tsien	虔	k'ien	製	ch	趨	ts'ü
覆	fuh	塵	ch'eng	尋	ts'ing	鑄	chu	赴	fu

10.

Corpses with titles, barren mandarins,
Some covet bliss and sacrifice to Budh,
Of their Pharisee (2) friends,
The wheel, they should look-at, upturned[g].

Husbandmen.

11.

In clay and mud running and walking,
I stealthy recognize the farmer ploughman,
At the pools irrigating, in the mists planting,
Brushing-off the dews, and trampling the dust

12.

In suburban grounds, he gathers and stores,
The *fruits* of successive (2) thick abundance,
In the furrow meditates, dreads judgment,
Bending knees, and piously seeks.

Artisans.

13.

Wield the foot-*rule*, whirl the pound-*axe*,
Are boastful of heroic steps[h],
Bows, arrows, vessels, materials,
Fine and coarse, they manufacture or cast.

Merchants.

14.

They refund prices, exhaust payments,
Fountain knives[i] surround on-either-hand,
IF they should-reflect on the final end,
With connected steps, they would run and go.

15 商客	16	17 居家	18	19 服官
市 sh	倍 pe	嘉 kia	刻 k'ah	卜 poh
隅 yü	億 yih	戚 ts'ih	薄 poh	賢 hien
井 tsing	典 tien	看 k'an	肇 chau	徵 cheng
際 tsi	掌 chang	承 ch'eng	衰 shwai	哲 cheh
買 mai	貢 kung	昆 kwan	憐 lien	荷 ho
賣 mai	稅 shŏe	玉 yü	惜 sih	政 cheng
客 k'ah	殷 ing	姊 ts	奴 nu	輸 shu
商 shang	繁 fan	妹 me	婢 pi	忠 chung
卻 k'ioh	錢 ts'ien	純 süin	普 p'u	俘 fu
迎 ying	滿 man	孝 hiau	護 hu	叛 p'an
巖 yai	慮 li	爺 ye	根 keng	禦 yü
島 tau	攘 jang	懽 hwan	源 yüen	盜 tau
坦 t'an	駐 chu	卑 pe	康 k'ang	驗 yien
坷 k'o	庫 k'u	弱 joh	寧 ning	印 ing
江 kiang	穹 k'iung	佑 yiu	允 yüing	頒 pan
洋 yang	蒼 ts'ang	惠 hwe	慰 we	封 fung

15.
At the market corner at the well's brink,
Buying and selling is the stranger merchant,
He rejects[j] or welcomes precipitous islands,
The smooth or rough of rivers or oceans.

16.
Double, ten-fold, he counts[k] in his palm,
Tributes and duties are vast and numerous,
Of money full, they think-of theft—
Locate your treasury in the concave azure.

The Family.

17.
Worthy relatives, see acceptance,
Brother gems, elder-sister and younger,
Pure filial piety, a father delights-in,
The humble and weak, protects, comforts.

18.
Meanness (2) begins decay,
Be-kind and sparing to slaves and maids,
Widely defend the root and fountain,
Tranquillity and peace will be secure.

Officers.

19.
They divine the virtuous, test the worthy,
Bearing government, repay fidelity[i],
They capture the rebel, restrain the robber,
Examine the stamp, distribute the seals.

	20		21 行善		22		23 悔罪		24
賓	ping	崗	kang	偏	p'ien	謹	king	戾	li
吏	li	磐	p'an	側	tsah	恪	k'ioh	綱	wang
阻	tsu	晨	ch'eng	陸	luh	密	mih	橫	hung
蔽	pi	屈	kiai	奠	tien	盟	ming	罹	li
釁	hing	湖	hu	圮	k'i	譽	yü	昌	ch'ang
詰	kih	漢	han	壞	hwai	賞	shang	衢	k'ü
覿	miau	星	sing	岸	an	似	s	閉	pi
躬	kung	遷	ts'ien	堅	kien	赫	hah	塞	sah
侯	s.	延	yien	那	na	輾	chüan	抱	pau
駕	kia	骰	ku	肯	k'eng	眼	yien	恨	heng
奏	tseu	藥	yoh	鬬	teu	崩	pang	沉	ch'eng
職	chih	送	sung	隙	hih	麗	hung	淪	lun
曷	hoh	需	sü	燕	wu	驚	king	況	kw'ang
厭	yien	飢	ki	穢	hwe	覬	tu	兼	kien
寬	kw'an	糧	liang	侵	tsing	幽	yiu	殘	ts'an
宏	hung	捐	kün	牽	k'ien	黑	heh	賊	tseh

20.
If guests or subordinates hinder and obrtruct
"The fault seek in *my* unworthy person" [m]
They wait the chariot report *their* office,
How *can we* weary of magnanimous officers?

Good Works.

21.
Hill and cliff, *with* dawn *they* arrive-at,
The Lake and Han, by the stars pass-over,
To prolong age, medicine *they* present,
For needy hunger, provision contribute.

22.
Uneven sideling ground *they* settle,
Tumbling decaying banks they strengthen,
Whence WOULD they fight and quarrel
Dirt and filth provoke and draw.

Retribution.

23.
Cautious, dignified, scrupulous in covenant,
Their praises and rewards seem dazzling,
In the turning of an eye, they fall and die,
And dread to behold gloom and darksness.

24.
Guilt's net, perveresely encounter,
The prosperous road is closed, stopped-up,
Hugging vain regrets they sink-down (2),
Much-more *who* combine cruelty and theft.

25 偽教	26	27 設	28 譬	29
邪 sie 黨 tang 毒 tuh 蛇 she	嫁 kia 怨 yüen 仗 chang 威 we	板 pan 柱 chu 瓦 wa 塔 t'ah	狂 kw'ang 犬 k'üen 虐 nioh 鄰 ling	房 fang 舍 she 樓 leu 臺 t'ai
領 ling 部 pu 吞 t'eng 噬 sh	鳴 ming 鼓 ku 暮 mo 季 ki	僅 king 彰 chang 樣 yang 制 ch	剛 kang 忿 fen 姑 ku 遜 süin	只 ts 堪 k'an 住 chu 宿 suh
舌 sheh 蜜 mih 售 sheu 甘 kan	濱 ping 退 t'e 崙 lŭn 逾 yü	帶 tai 繫 hi 帕 p'a 懸 hüen	放 fang 膽 tan 裸 lo 腹 fuh	獅 sh 駝 t'o 牲 seng 禽 k'ing
煨 hwo 虜 lo 倚 i 勢 sh	奈 nai 寡 kwa 頂 ting 替 t'i	零 ling 珍 chen 表 piau 餙 shih	毛 mau 髮 fah 謗 pang 刺 ts'	象 siang 狀 chwang 閃 shan 突 t'uh

The Malicious.

25.
Corrupt cliques, venemous serpents,
Lead companies to swallow, and devour,
Their tongues honey, *they* sell sweet *words*,
Destroy capture, and rest on force.

26.
They vent spleen and rely on power,
He shall sound the drum at evening season[n]—
From the brink retire, the mountain overleap,
(0) Few[o] *will* bear *the duty in your* stead.

The Superficial.

27.
Board pillars, and tile towers,
Merely exhibit the pattern decreed;
The belt to bind, the kerchief to suspend,
Have scattered pearls for outside ornaments.

28.
Rabid dogs oppress their neighbors—
To their hard rage, gently yield,
They let-out gall[p] and bare their bellies,
But a hair *displaced* (2) slander and pierce,

29.
House cottage, loft or terrace[q],
We only can dwell-in for a night's-lodging,
Lions, camels, cattle and birds,
Emblems form, in motions sudden.

30	31	32	33	34
回耶 憶穌				
移 i	屢 le	竆 tsien	嚴 yien	囊 nang
磨 mo	憶 i	枝 ch'	防 fang	綻 chan
蘇 su	釘 ting	撻 t'ah	假 kia	麻 ma
蟲 ch'ung	痛 t'ung	打 ta	酵 kiau	補 pu
燃 jan	竟 king	渴 k'oh	暫 chan	菓 ko
燈 teng	斃 ts'ien	擬 i	辭 ts'	咒 cheu
照 chau	戈 ko	鹽 yien	慄 lih	葉 yeh
瞽 ku	鋒 fung	充 ch'ung	杯 pe	肥 fe
忙 mang	棘 kih	腓 fe	鸞 yuh	索 soh
愧 kwe	冠 kwan	骨 kuh	鴿 koh	騎 k'i
錯 ts'oh	頭 t'eu	慢 man	遁 tun	橄 kan
差 ch'a	戴 tai	折 cheh	院 yuen	欖 lan
仰 niang	袍 pau	寵 ch'ung	捕 p'u	到 tau
慕 mo	片 p'ien	壽 sheu	魚 yü	郇 süing
觀 king	搖 yau	旋 süin	射 she	管 kwan
附 fu	紅 hung	增 tseng	圉 we	吹 ch'öe

30.
Move a milstone, and you wake insects,
Kindle a lamp, you enlighten the blind.
Make-haste *to be* ashamed of faults (2)
Aspire (2) to see and be-united *with* God.

Remembrance of Christ.

31.
Oft remember the nail's pain—
Christ at-last expired *at the* weapon's point,
The thorny crown, his head bore,
His robe skirts waved red.

32.
They clipped a branch to scourge and strike,
Thirsty, decreed him the briny *cup*-full,
His leg bones, *they were* slow to break—
Favor and age in-turn were added'.

33.
He sternly cautioned against false leaven,
For-a-short-time declined the trembling cup,
Sellers of doves fled the court,
Catchers of fish shot around.

34.
The sack rent, flax must mend',
The fruit-tree cursed *had* leaves fat,
They sought *a beast* to ride to Olivet (2)
Coming-to Zion trumpets (tubes) were-blown

ANALYTICAL READER.

35 正教	36 傳宣	
振 chin	朔 soh	
枯 k'u	夏 hia	
拔 p'ah	盤 p'an	
草 ts'au	蹈 tau	

宥 yiu	核 heh
勇 yung	斗 teu
伸 sheng	辨 pien
囚 ts'iu	州 cheu

苗 miau	暨 ki
絲 hi	寒 han
齊 ts'i	迄 k'ih
魯 lu	熱 jeh

品 p'ing	曳 yeh
格 koh	杖 chang
呂 lü	緯 we
歐 eu	球 k'iu

凡五百七十六字

35.

He revives the withered, plucks the grass,
Pardons the brave, enlarges the prisoner,
His original race *are but as* Ts'i and Lu,—
All classes come to *service*, Lü and Eu'.

Apostles of the Faith.

36.

North and South, by the compass they tread,
Compare the pole-star to distinguish lands,
Through extreme cold, and extreme heat,
They drag the staff and girdle they globe.

NOTES.

a. Lit. *doubts*, but according to classic precedent used here for 擬 *to decide a doubt.*
b. Lit. *Snows*, allays the burning wrongs.
c. The Powers of Darkness.
d. Lit. *Push*, i.e. push the comparison, 類推
e. Lit. matter, substance.
f. Scil. falling into the above named faults.
g. i.e. take warning.
h. Lofty climbing.
i. Money, so called from the shape of ancient coin. 泉 is often used as a synonym for 錢
j. i.e. leaves.
k. Lit. To rule or manage. 典 a rule or canon.
l. Repay favor with fidelity. 輸 also means defeat.
m. The language of a good officer, who makes himself responsible.
n. Denounce them at the evening of time, the end of the world.
o. Reformation is a personal affair.
p. Used for courage or audacity.

q. Great pains are taken with external things while the heart is left in the condition described in the next verse.

It is not easy to discover the pertinence of several expressions in this part of the chapter, but let it be remembered, they were put together merely for the purpose of using up a residuum of characters for which no place could be found elsewhere.

r. Isaiah 53.10.
s. Luke 5. 36.
t. With him all nations are alike, and all classes numbered among his followers. Lü, the family name of Kiang T'ai kung, Eu, Euyang Siu; the one celebrated for military, the other for literary genius, and here employed to represent two grand divisions of society.

Since the previous pages were printed, the following has been suggested as an improved reading for part of verse 29.

牲駝狀象　禽閃獅突

Cows and camels form emblems, Birds dart, lions *leap* suddenly,

牲 is chiefly used for sacrificial beasts, which may very properly be said to form emblems; though the emblematic character of the camel is not quite so clear.

CHAPTER IV.

ANALYTICAL READER

第四章論儔類 — ti s chang lan ch'eu le

總冒

1. 緬迹溯勳 — mien, tsih, su, hüing
儘鮮缺漏 — tsing, süin, k'üih, leu
擲畀某儔 — chih, pi, mo, ch'eu
搴裳參叩 — k'ien, shang, ts'an, k'eu

2. 模楷秘探 — mo, k'ie, pi, t'an
煩劇暢茂 — fan, kü, ch'ang, meu
殆冀瞶聾 — tai, ki, kw'e, lung
僉懺誤謬 — ts'ien, ch'an, wu, miu

天文

3. 晴嵐縈繞 — ts'ing, nan, liau, jiau
瞻矙層霄 — chan, chuh, ts'un, siau
霞輝林豔 — hia, hwe, ling, yien
霓彩渡消 — ni, ts'ai, tu, siau

4. 迅雷奮響 — süing, le, feng, hiang
疏霜催凋 — su, shuang, ch'ue, tiau
暘霽旱潦 — yang, ing, han, lau
竚覿變調 — chu, tih, sih, t'iau

CHAPTER IV.

MISCELLANEOUS TOPICS,

1.

In connected steps trace *the Creator's* merit,
Very rare are its defects" (2),
He cast-forth and gave each-*thing its* class,
Tuck-up clothes, together knock *the head.*

2.

Of model forms*,* the mystery if you fathom,
Perplexing sorely *is* their full abundance,
You almost expect the blind and deaf,
All to repent their mistakes and errors.

Meteorology.

3.

The clear air encircles *us,*
We gaze attentive on the storied vault,
The sunset's* lustre *has* a forest of beauties,
The rainbow splendor passes-over and melts,

4.

Swift thunder* fiercely echoes,
The herb, frost hastens to wither,
The bright and cloudy, drought and flood,
Place face-to-face, *Nature's* Alchemist *(2).

5 地理		6		7 時令		8		9 山水	
攷	k'au	悞	wu	辯	pien	靜	tsing	岱	tai
究	kiu	歧	k'i	辰	ch'eng	占	chan	嶽	yoh
寰	hwan	徑	king	訝	yia	晏	yien	欽	k'ing
區	k'ü	抄	ch'au	午	wu	曉	hiau	嶷	i
長	ch'ang	併	ping	驟	tseu	熾	ch'	渭	we
短	tŭan	程	ch'eng	閱	yüih	燄	yien	川	ch'uan
闊	kw'eh	堑	chan	春	ch'ün	爍	sheh	迢	t'iau
狹	hiah	劃	hwah	秋	ts'iu	硫	liu	遞	ti
凸	kung	盪	tang	雙	shwang	璣	ki	鑒	tsoh
凹	au	疆	kiang	尢	wan	衡	heng	險	hien
崎	k'i	拓	toh	踯	chih	驗	yien	覓	mih
嶇	k'ü	輿	yü	躅	chuh	算	sŭan	津	tsing
函	ping	蠻	man	晷	kwe	怒	ts'ung	陟	chih
燕	yien	貊	meh	逝	shi	遽	kü	涉	sheh
崖	yai	包	pau	影	ing	蹴	ch'u	攀	p'an
峽	hiah	刮	kwah	浮	feu	躊	ch'eu	躋	tsi

Geography.

5.

Search, explore, the circle of space,
The long and short, broad and narrow,
Bulged and sunken, rough and uneven,
Ping's and Yien's, cliffs and passes.

6.

The erring bye-way, a path *may* rectify',
The urgent journey, a precipice interrupt,
In laying boundaries, and opening territories,
Barbarous and savage *were* embraced (2).

Time.

7.

We talk a morning, and are startled by noon,
We gallop over spring and autumn;
The twin orbs jog-on (2),
And on the dial, the passing shadow floats.

8.

Quietly observe evening and morning,
Swift as kindling flame or flashing sulphur,
Globe and transverse' verify calculation,
Rapidly, suddenly *Time* rushes-on (2).

Hills and Waters.

9.

The Tai Mountains *are* lofty and eminent,
Across the We stream *is* a distant reach,
Travellers chisel steeps to find crossings,
They mount, wade, cling, and climb.

67 — ANALYTICAL READER

10	11 人品	12	13 宮室	14
嶂 chang 翠 ts'ue 排 p'ai 螺 lo	髻 t'iau 僮 t'ung 耆 k'i 耇 keu	顢 man 頇 han 伶 ling 俐 li	畫 hwa 榭 sie 雕 tiau 廊 lang	齋 chai 墊 shuh 序 sü 庫 ts'iang
潮 ch'au 黃 hwang 駛 sh 驥 ki	倜 t'ih 儻 t'ang 俠 hiah 豪 hau	縷 lu 晰 sih 膚 fu 毫 hau	複 fuh 堦 kiai 夾 kiah 牖 yiu	廩 ling 廚 ch'u 厠 s 厩 kiu
玄 hüin 幻 hwan 巧 k'iau 臻 cheng	遴 ling 薦 tsien 勵 li 獎 tsiang	胞 pau 胚 p'e 配 p'e 締 t'i	斐 fe 檻 k'ien 聯 lien 帛 mien	衍 yien 慶 k'ing 迓 yia 休 hiu
佳 kia 玩 wan 攸 yiu 寄 ki	諂 ch'an 傲 au 譏 ki 嘲 ch'an	妙 miau 奧 au 頗 p'o 饒 jau	綺 i 窗 chw'ang 輻 fuh 輳 ts'eu	恥 ch' 玷 tien 楣 me 構 keu

10.

The summits green *are* ranged *like* sea-shells,
The tide yellow wafts galleys,
Mysterious changes! skill extreme!
Noble enjoyments *are* therein conveyed.

Classes of Men.

11.

The uncombed lad, the bald greybeard,
The careless (2) the daring, the generous,
Selected for promotion, stimulated by praise,
Flatterers, proud, cynics and scorners.

12.

The stupid (2) and sprightly (2),
Are distinguished skin and hair,
From the womb (2) fitted and designed—
Admirable mysteries (0) abound!

Palaces and Houses.

13.

Have painted banisters, carved verandahs,
Double stair-ways, opposite windows,
Elegant railings joined together,
Gauze window-panes in clusters (2).

14.

Studio, school, academy and college,
Garner, kitchen, privy, stable.
Prolong felicity, *and* welcome good-fortune,
A shameful *act* will stain the door-post (2).

ANALYTICAL READER — 69

服飾		器用		珍寶
15	16	17	18	19
葛 koh 裘 k'iu 絺 ch' 綌 hih	衒 hüin 耀 yau 襟 king 袖 siu	聶 heh 舥 ku 評 p'ing 材 ts'ai	揮 hwe 塵 chu 挽 waṇ 韁 kiang	寸 ts'un 珠 chu 咫 ts 璧 pih
簪 tsan 珥 r 鐲 choh 鐶 hwan	掩 yien 映 ing 副 fu 鑲 siang	借 tsie 資 ts 佐 tso 輔 fu	吮 yüing 筆 pih 裁 ts'ai 楮 tu	青 ts'ing 珩 heng 丹 tan 瑚 hu
錦 king 披 p'i 繡 siu 佩 p'e	髦 mau 齡 ling 限 hien 促 ts'oh	睡 shwe 眠 mien 榻 t'ah 牀 chw'ang	妥 t'o 貯 chu 穩 wen 儲 ch'u	洛 loh 鐘 chung 泗 s 磬 k'ing
燦 ts'an 爛 lan 煇 hwe 煌 hwan	徨 hwan 戀 lien 裝 chwang 潢 hwang	甕 yung 瘈 sün 匕 pi 筯 chu	般 pan 件 kien 艫 lu 署 shu	秦 ts'in 鼎 ting 唐 t'ang 鑪 lu

Clothes and Ornaments.

15.
Linen, fur, silk, and hemp,
Hair-pin, pendant, bracelet, ring,
Gilded cloak, embroidered side-piece[g],
Sparkling, bright, brilliant, splendid.

16.
Dazzling radiant skirts and sleeves,
Veil the image with borders[h] and fringes;
When age (2) *is so* limited and brief,
What-liesure *is there* to dote-on dress (2)!

Vessels and Utensils.

17.
Distinguish vessels, criticise their material,
Borrow *them as* means to aid and assist,
We slumber and sleep on couch and bed,
Breakfast and sup with spoon and chopstick.

18.
Flourish the whip (brush), grasp the rein,
Tongue[i] the pen, trim the paper.
Safely store, securely provide,
Each kind and piece record in-order.

Precious Stones.

19.
The inch pearl, the span diamond,
Green emerald, red coral,
The Luh bell, the Sze harp,
Ts'in tripod, T'ang censer[j].

20	21 音樂	22	23 花木	25
琳 ling	噓 hü	湍 t'ŭan	脂 ch	桃 t'au
瑯 lang	竹 chuh	激 kih	妍 yien	李 li
琥 hu	彈 t'an	峯 fung	粉 fen	競 king
玖 kiu	絲 s	迴 hwe	媚 me	暖 n'ŭan
碼 ma	簫 siau	霹 t'ing	秀 siu	松 sung
瑙 nau	韶 chau	轟 hung	麗 li	栢 peh
砥 wu	拊 fu	電 tien	崑 chŭan	耐 nai
砆 fu	拍 p'eh	掣 ch'eh	鍾 chung	冬 tung
峻 tsun	逸 yih	賡 tsih	黛 tai	趁 ch'eng
嶸 yung	韻 yüing	詠 yung	痕 heng	候 heu
璀 ts'ŭe	鏗 k'eng	翕 hih	楊 yang	釀 niang
璨 ts'an	鏘 ts'iang	諧 yai	柳 liu	景 king
醞 weng	淋 ling	濫 lan	綠 luh	苑 yüen
孕 yüing	鈴 ling	竽 yü	蔭 ing	囿 yiu
含 han	裂 lih	羞 siu	梧 wu	酣 han
娛 wu	帛 peh	測 ts'ah	桐 t'ung	融 yung

20.

Ling and lang*ᵏ*, amber and ebony,
Cornelian (2) and agate (2),
Magnificent (2) and sparkling (2)—
Pregnant (2) contain enjoyment.

Sounds and Music.

21.

Puff the bamboo, beat the silk-thread,
Flute the Shau, press *holes* touch *keys*—
Pleasure's rhymes *softly* jingle (2),
The Ling-ling (2) *sounds like* tearing silk.

22.

The billow's dash, the cliff turns-back,
Thunder booms, lightning flashes—
Concert singing *must be* harmonious (2),
The seeming piper *is* ashamed-of discovery*ˡ*.

Flowers and Trees.

23.

As the rouged beauty or starched belle,
Blooming, elegant, specially favored,
Are the dark shadowed willow (2),
And the green shaded wut'ung (2).

24.

The peach and pear improve by warmth,
The fir and cypress endure winter.
Profiting-by the season, ripening into beauty,
Garden and park intoxicate with harmony.

蔬菜				鱗介	
25	26	27 鳥獸	28	29	
飽 pau	掇 chŭeh	騰 t'eng	雞 ki	鱗 ling	
飫 yü	擷 kih	祥 ts'iang	塒 sh	介 kiai	
芳 fang	鬱 yuh	毓 yuh	豚 t'un	蕃 fan	
馨 hing	芬 fen	瑞 shŭe	柵 chah	滋 ts	
蓺 i	咀 tsü	鳳 fung	鴻 hung	譜 p'u	
畝 mu	嚼 tsoh	鬐 tu	渚 tu	題 t'i	
蓄 hioh	彌 mi	麟 ling	鵲 ts'ioh	鼉 ts'u	
菜 ts'ai	快 kw'ai	遨 au	巢 ch'au	碓 k'ioh	
剖 p'o	胡 hu	驊 hwa	鰵 siu	龜 kwe	
瓜 kwa	羨 sien	騮 liu	餌 r	鼈 pih	
採 ts'ai	腥 sing	馳 ch'	敷 fu	黿 yüen	
薇 we	羶 shan	騁 ch'eng	豫 yü	鼉 t'o	
煮 chu	饌 chŭang	鸞 lŭan	詎 kü	鯤 kw'en	
葵 kw'e	肴 hiau	鶴 hoh	歔 kih	鰲 ao	
拾 shih	儵 ch'	翔 ts'iang	烹 p'eng	鯨 k'ing	
芥 kiai	泰 t'ai	翺 au	庖 p'au	鱷 oh	

Herbs and Vegetables.

25.
Full fed on fragrant aroma,
Work your acres, store your herbs,
Divide the melon, pluck the pot-plant,
Boil the sun-flower, gather mustard.

26.
Pick and break, the confined fragrance,
Chewing (2) increases pleasure,
Why long for stenches and odors,
Meats and viands, profuse, extravagant?

Birds and Beasts.

27.
Mounting prosperity, brooding good-luck,
The phœnix soars. The kiling roams,
The horse (2) runs and gallops,
The lûan and sea-eagle gyrate and hover.

28.
Chickens *live in* coops, pigs *in* styes (crates),
Geese on sand-banks, magpies in nests;
Their food (2) *is* spread ready—
Who *is* anxious *what* to bake in kitchen[m]?

Fishes.

29.
The scaly-tribe (2) numerous swarms,
The record themes *are* plain and reliable,
Tortoise, terrapin, turtle (2),
kwen, au, (2) whale and shark[n].

30	31 昆嵐	32	33 預終	34
淬蝗掬鰕 sṅe hwang kṅih hia	蠶織蛛組 ts'an chih chu tsu	抛攊獵蟻 p'au lṅan lieh i	罷勉肅雍 ming mien suh yung	涕淚悚惶 t'i le sung hwang
泅雀撈蛤 ts'iu ts'ioh lau koh	蚓唱蟬吟 ying ch'ang ch'ang ying	摶飯鬨蠅 t'uan fan hung ing	慌逢殤殂 hwang fung shang tsu	頻摯伴侶 p'ing hih pan lü
卵濕累孳 lṅan sh le ts	徜徉遂閣 t'ang yang sue koh	么麽瞬盼 yau mo shun p'an	軀殼匪牢 k'ü k'uh fe lau	旦肆旬諏 tan i süin tseu
俄頃跳躍 o k'ing t'iau yoh	紬繹開庭 ch'eu yih hien t'ing	罔忖淒辛 wang ts'un ts'i sing	靑悶酸楚 tsing t'ah snan ts'u	警惕臭腐 king t'ih hiu fu

30.

It plunges a locust, and you pick-up a crab,
It swims a sparrow, you clutch an oyster.
Their eggs in moisture frequent multiply,
In-a-moment (2) they leap and spring°.

Insects.

31.

The silk-worm weaves, the spider knits,
The earth-worm sings, the beetle hums,
Spread-through (2) suites of galleries,
Interwoven (2) in vacant halls.

32.

Throw-down meat, you catch ants,
Knead boiled-rice, then buz the flies—
Little-things! a moment they look-about,
But do-not think-of grief and bitterness^p.

Memento Mori.

33.

Be earnest (2) reverential, composed,
Suddenly to meet decease and dissolution,
This corporeal shell is-not firm,
Faults and offences are sour and painful.

34.

With trickling tears and anxious dread,
Often lead *your* associates (2),
Each morning urge, *each* decade exhort them,
To respect and seriousness *in view* of decay.

ANALYTICAL READER

敀
35 格

紹 sheng
窺 kw'e
浩 hau
蕩 t'ang

喧 hüin
奕 yih
无 wu
邊 pien

緝 ts'ih
熙 hi
淵 yüen
穆 muh

翹 k'iau
睇 t'i
鈞 küing
顏 yien

36
俛 fu
匐 fuh
跣 si
跟 ki

憨 ch'an
懋 te
胥 sü
刪 shan

嶇 eu
僂 leu
赲 ts'uh
蹃 tsih

冥 ming
頑 wan
徐 ts'ü
悛 chün

效
37 德

策 ts'ah
絜 hih
臣 ch'eng
僚 liau

禹 yü
湯 t'ang
堯 yau
舜 shun

箴 cheng
規 kwe
紳 sheng
儒 ju

仲 chung
閔 ming
孔 k'ung
孟 mung

38
斟 chen
酌 choh
奢 shai
淳 süen

雙 shuang
甄 cheng
標 piau
準 chǔn

炎 yien
火 ho
怖 pu
燒 shau

撫 fu
膺 ing
敏 ming
懇 k'eng

凡六百八字

Exhortation.

35.
Much-more pry-into the vast grand *mystery*,
Its noise is great without bound,
Brilliant (2) profound, sublime,
Upward look-to the venerable face^q.

36.
Stooping, creeping, bare-foot, kneeling,
Ashamed, vexed, wholly purging away *evil*.
Bowing down, (2) with reverence (2),
The dark and stupid gradually reform.

Virtue and Vice.

37.
To spur and lead officers (2),
Point-to Yu, T'ang, Yau and Shun^r;
For maxims and rules, the belted scholar,
Takes Tslu, Mingts, Confucius, Mencius^s.

38.
Reflect-on (2) excéss and purity,
Of the twain distinguish mark and aim^t,
Flaming fire *will* consume (2) *the vicious*^u—
Beating the breast, earnestly entreat^v.

Notes.

a. Lit. gaps and leaks.
b. The forms designed by the Creator, each the model of a class.
c. 霞 The evening aurora, the *abendrothe* of the Germans.
d. 燮 To temper with heat, and 調 to change transform or stir, taken together express the operations of the chemist.
e. Lit. to copy, hence to correct in copying, also to take or attain by a more direct road.
f. Lit. transverse, a balance, but in connexion with 璣 on astronomical instrument of whose form we are not very certain.
g. 佩 To carry at the side; any thing worn at the side.
h. 副 Secondary or subordinate, used for the border of a garment.
i. 舐 To touch with the tongue, as a Chinese scribe does, to adjust the point of his pen.
j. 寶石 The Chinese title of this verse comprehends two classes. The antique articles named in the last two lines belong to the first class.
洛 泗 Names of rivers, 秦 唐 Names of dynasties.
k. In some uncertainty as to these stones, it seems preferable to retain the native names.
l. *Shau* and *Lingling* in verse 21. are names of musical compositions. In verse 22. the sounds of nature are represented as imitated in music. The "seeming piper" was one who sought to pass for a musician, by imitating the motions of others in the band, but without hazarding a note.
m. Mat. vi. 26.
n. As *kwen* and *au* are names of fabulous monsters, it will hardly be admitted that the ichthyology of the Chinese is "plain and reliable".
o. 累 "frequent" has the double sense of the Latin *frequens*. Locusts are believed to turn to crabs, and sparrows to oysters.
p. They live a moment free from cares. The musical powers of the earthworm are confidently asserted.
q. "Noise" in a good sense, for fame. Face, the face of God.
r. Ancient emperors.
s. Philosophers.
t. 標 An object aimed at, 準 a line to guide by.

PART. III.

ANALYSIS OF CHARACTERS.

常 字 雙 千 合 釋

CONSTANT CHARACTERS, A COUPLE OF THOUSANDS—ANALYZED.

NOTE.

The "elements" are of two kinds—perfect and imperfect. Of the former, many are found in the table of radicals, and others occur in the text. The rest, together with the imperfect elements, are arranged in a list at the end of this Part, according to the chapters in which they occur.

千雙字常

遂口一	孚烏巫矢	卩処易土	白白八
八禾十	月爪靁厶	人虍貝其	ノ一比㠯

遂亦和土　將為靈矣　命處賜基　千百皆與

八口 / 工一 / 亻 …（偏旁拆字）

六日力作　先闢天地　萬物多焉　既希且異

木一氏木 / 牛口从 / 刖月一巾 / 屮卜䒑 / 几群大也 / 禹勿夕㞢 / 廾牛夕正 / 旡 / 白匕布一共 / ㄨ月田

未生民來　前有上帝　惟一真神　無聖能比

隹八申 / 小勿直示 / 呈匕耳肙匕

第一章　論古始

常字雙千編韻一名認字新法

呼丂考同口音圉

其禁令而自取罪戾哉、疾羊切孚音律
自音怨亠音頭ノ音䰜ㄨ厶五古文𠘧
譌同靈ㄙ音私虍音

右第一節記上主造物之多所以備人之用也人奈何犯

告云可食 或當見耳 聞言摩拿 得罪因此
牛二丁人 戈尚目 門言麻合 千四口止
日厶口良 一田儿 耳口手手 𡨄非大匕
ㄧ个一 犬欠口 王㤙
八斤曰 勹谷羊心 耳又
儿戶丱 火欠口
一六一

凡所求者 毋不立予 然欲善惡 勿聽手取
儿戶丱 勹一 犬欠口 耳壬㤙
八斤曰 一六一 勹谷羊 王
一个一 丱生 口言 找口目
弓ノ女ノ

復使宜家 女兮徃事 謂之曰夫 爾我如自
复吏且豕 弓生 胃一人 找口目
千亻山山 八亻 言口二 ノ女ノ

千雙字常

惡墜					
中傳亞伯	亻專 口亻 •亻	丨 白	以致彼族	义皮 至亻 方人	爻意非昔	八心 音	卷撒全死	夫扌 人王 一 死

83

夫扌人王 — 卷撒全死 — 爻意非昔 — 以致彼族 — 惡墜中傳亞伯

亻可口亻門亻君 — 何問儕羣 — 共二日 — 旦女彳山禾夕 — 但安利名 — 亦言灬亻 — 羊祭信心

竹亻止亦、艹 — 第歸方蓋 — 甲口十寺日 — 即由是時 — 必彐尸刀 — 愛身尼色 — 一右儿艹口 — 長子若兒

貝亻門一口羊 — 則同義人 — 人口行亻 — 大水四行 — 歹彳維一余 — 列馬羅金 — 夊父糸 — 敵殺及今

救降

故又督教　甚加世福　降下耶穌　斯實救主

攵目攵　古叔孝　甘力世祈　ト一耳魚　其山求、

匹口一畐　夅卜ㄅ禾　ㄣㄠ攵王　斤貫攵

同弔邑堆本字冂音肩

有八人從七者所携潔畜牝牡各七也事見創世記、一音

矣尼噫也僕謂挪亞也方蓋方舟也居八者挪亞眷屬共　裒邪

洪水横行上主實惡其汚穢也、非有義人則人類幾絕滅

右第二節記世人之犯禁墮惡殘殺貪暴造孽日深所以

古　尸从　口立

八比　彳　攵扌

居八從七　各拉入門

千雙字常

土溫雅　　　　一　土　溫　隹
　　　　　　　　　　氵　牙
王而溫雅　　　　　　　炙
後章昭諸　　　　千　早　召
　　　　　　　　　立　日　者
冷迦城邑　　　　　言
巴米道路
猶太國也　　　令之成巴
西乃山乎　　　　　加　土口
　　　　　　　　　八　首　足
目勻你一　　　　　　　　猶
木糹四十　　　　　木之各　　或
　　　　　　　　　　犬大口
心口里夂
ノ矢王叟
　　　　　　　　即豐寸去
相約眾士　　　　竹而山氵
必知理數
節禮守法
司十二徒

寺日　　　　　侖山於二
竹門　　　　　亻山方力

等間于三　　　　華
　　　　　　　　艹
倫出於五　　　　　　　　土夂
　　　　　　　　　　　　　展
華年至殿

在會受書

凡二百四十字

亠音綿畢音必氺音吟夊音逡

出世誕育於人也事載新約福音書後章即詳其事、_{古文}
在三位之中居於第二也倫出於五者耶穌雖爲神子、_{夅降}
自救故特降下愛子爲萬世之救主也等間于三者耶穌
右第三節記上主降救之故蓋深憫世人迷於惡途不能

常字雙千

書同古迴字背備本字厤曆本字自音堆厂音漢㬎音蜆殷音聲

右第一節總冒下文此章之綱領也幕喻身也見彼得後

| 背止古佯 頁力力力 | 一刀 |
| 厤卄英 㬎戈工㬎 | 一川女日 |

備歷苦難　顯成功勞　追厥本初　垂訓汝曹

| 見昌巾 | 文之丞之 | 家之弋賣 | 耳𣎳血同 |
| 亲䘮其 | 赤㡭扌兆 | 卄㬎亻貝 | 殷禾𠆢㚅 |

親營皮幕　赦過拯逃　蒙選代贖　聲稱益高

領綱

第二章　論教化

常字雙千編韻字新法
一名認

軍光星光也、珵音確糸音覺

右第二節記耶穌出世之初、天卽垂象而先顯示於人也、

造室辱臨　伏拜依次

曾緣夢感　忽產男嗣　東界友師　軍光詳視

母氏瑟妻　少小待字　蓮容素端　蘭性較細

日象夕心　八糸芇咸　心ノ力刂　勿立田口　曰田ナ自　木介又巾　一小言示　車元羊見　軍光交田　閞生交田　廾廾車糸

至寸人品　告山辰臣　乀衣欠　亻亻丶　犬

必一改　珏　ノ寺子　小千山　廾運谷糸峀　廾山主立

出世

千雙字常

穌也、繆音六开音堅彡音衫充音留巩音拱
空也畜老則毛脫而皮空喻希律旣髦而行惡也龍謂耶
右第三節記耶穌嬰時遭害備極苦難而始得安全也荒

畜老革荒　龍現首舉　免歟幸哉　原靡終始

田匕十免　　　　　龍見自手　　兇欠羊戈　　　小非冬台
玄歹卅廿　　　　　音王宀與　　刀與土吉　　　厂麻糸女

辶口十夂　　十目之一　　　乃心力口　　　夕架兒厶
台尹宀氵　　宏八反又上　　衣氵月土

追君卒沒　率眷返止　仍恐勒召　夜深脫去

口王取心　　　　　安尸戈刂　　那貝父之　　辶竟臧彡
戶白曰刄　　　　　扌一繆开　　扌刀扌袁　　辟土卄开

時嬰
后皇最忍　　按戶劓刑　　挪負投遠　　避境藏形

洗				試				
愛			見					

右第四節、記耶穌受洗之事河約但河也越過也

向	同	譬	言	嘗	旨	拜	开	
野	予	樹	壹	過	之	令	人	府
翰	人	結	古	魔	鬼	俯	亡	玉
呼	乎	果	木	試	式	望	月	

				指	旨	尊	酋	寸
悔	每	適	辵	餅	幷	榮	弓	木
改	已	口	隹	爭	食	強	方	雖
務	攵	維	商	遺	爪	施	人	也
切	力	悅	糸		貴			

				押	甲	修	彡	
就	尤	否	口	登	豆	德	做	口
洗	先	悉	心	宮	呂	圖	幸	及
河	河	刃	采	屋	至	報		一
旁	方	斷	刀					自

	盾	便	更	崇	宗	正	止	
循	義	付	寸	垣	亘	直	乙	
儀	大	焚	林	被	皮	兩	虍	
莫	戌	烈	列	擔	衣	虛	业	
越	走		火					

千雙字常

攵手𠂇𠂇
工𢀖韋𫝀

攻擊違逆　　　巾𣎎𠂈央　　䜌音㘽
尚取亻卄　　　阝日田卩　東

常聚俊英　　　日丶米貝

旨斥氣責　　　七斤气主

隱暗畢陳

道
宣
乘驢歡樂　　　恩木日心　　条戒長巾　辛台蜀口
　　　　　　　系隹知㗊　作言弓刀　山氵尸五

總集智愚

條誡張布

宰治屬吾

卒離之而去也，驢音俊𩢷音郎及音伏

右第五節、記耶穌見試之日為魔所逼而守正不阿、故魔

奉諭遵遣　　烏敢惑余

千俞之之　　攵心未
人入三　　　百或人
三言尊豈

孰 享 九
忘 亡 心
足 口 止
畏 田 𧘇

頓 屯 頁
害 宀 舌
體 骨 豊
魂 云 鬼

該 言 亥
侍 忄 寺
庇 广 比
釋 釆 睪

藉 廾 耒 昔
謝 言 射
恩 因 心
仁 亻 二

失 ノ 夫
懼 忄 瞿
災 巛 火
絶 糸 色

好 女 子
甲 曰 丨
亂 𤔔 乙
俱 亻 具

仇 亻 九
怒 奴 心
財 貝 才
據 扌 豦

兵 丘 八
奪 大 隹 寸
車 亘 丨
驅 馬 區

花 艹 化
嫩 女 敕
易 日 勿
敗 貝 攵

麥 來 人 夕
掃 扌 帚
定 宀 疋
留 卯 田

類 米 大 頁
反 厂 又
烏 一 烏
獸 嘼 犬

穀 𡉉 禾 殳
養 羊 食
弗 弓 ‖
憂 𦣻 夊

患 串 心
遭 曹 辶
獄 狺 犬
陷 阝 臽

謀 言 某
亡
沙 氵 少
洲 氵 州

統 糸 充
轄 車 害
的 白 勺
裔 衣 冏

征 彳 正
途 余 辶
遍 扁 辶
周 冂 吉

千雙字常

每十可男 　　　　　　　　　　業未之己
氵一可八 　　　　　　　　　　云业束走　復戈青之　頁隹卽土
　　　　　　　　　　　　　　　　　　　尸止言隋　原禸乡田

海干哥弟　棄業速起　履武請隨
　　　　　　　　　　　　　　　顧離鄉里

教　學別派支　埃田許置　敬妾艮分　詛禁祝極
立

子刂辰又　矣口午直　久女民刀　且示兄亞
另刂氵十　士十言四　荀亡一八　言林示木

聲罾畜古文巛川本字乙古文隱字屬同亂虔音渠广龕上聲
　　　　　　氣氣本字懸同隱昏遙上
　　　　　　　　　　龗音灌恩音聰芉逆本字

嬌好也類人類也好甲猶好兵也

悖教者謀訟耶穌而耶穌避去也的裔以色列之民也嫩

右第六節記耶穌宣道之時多言譬喻以教人也獄訟也

目紀矜恤	一已日糸	邦都省京	ㄗㄗ手目	燔牡割肉	番土火牛	私願公禱	ㄙ禾頁侖
	今血		者少		害人		八亓 壽
志揚讚美	心易土扌	南北半經	羊匕牜	舊例雖存	臼列隹	葡萄飲傾	++ ++ 匍匐
	贊言		門糸		子虽		欠食亻
	大羊		巠		仔		
默記祈文	心易	每念儳僞	母心	羔牛特犢	火十羊	開堂誠勸	門土
	土扌		一二		寺一		尙成
	黑言		亻亻		賣牛		言力
	示丶		替爲		牛		雚
通達古史	犬已斤又	化導平情	匕寸干靑	錫獻豈欣	金易犬山	引證宣音	弓言山立
	辶辶口		亻道八		虍豆		
	甫幸十		十		欠斤		一登亘日
	口						

千雙字常

詣船波面　息風舟底　愈疾環觀　活喪侍喜
　旨𦣞皮三　心虫丹氏　心矢睘見　舌寺廾口
　言舟氵而　自凡ノ广　兪广王𦘒　氵亻吉

鬼逐病醫　汚解禍滅　葬墓寝興　捫衣婦潔
　田豕广殹　丐𠬪咼戌　死茻宀同　扌門帶𫝀
　氵角亦氵　氵刀冎氵　歺莫山冂　才氵女氵

　允吾貝兪　可各又妥　頁重夂昜　月少
　亻言中口　大田曰扌　隹禾牛亻　戉止

奇行
　著語貴喻　奇畧更接　顧種牧傷　夕朝歲月
　也割肉割禮也　手音拜羊音徍膓音察
　　　　　　底派本字去音笑葉音葉

右第七節、記耶穌立教之正、改舊禮而用新禮也、武足跡

言　昔　夂
預　糸　扁　永
散　寅　貝　金　永
編　言　兌　亻　尹
賽　　　　　　　　夊
說　　　　　　　　于　土　夊
　　　　　　　　　　冉　山　予
　　　　錄　　　　及　一　言
　　　　久　　　　　　韭　一
　　　　兆　　　　毀　　　其
　　　　伊　　　　宇　白　　
　　　　　　　　　再　　　頁
　　　　　　　　　建　　　十
　　　　　　　　　　　　　木
喻　　　　　　　　　　　　月
耶　　　　　　　　　預　　
穌　　　　　　　　　計　　
也　　　　　　　　　末　　
、　亐今作于岊音跬威滅本字广音狀丝音幽　期　　

右第八節記耶穌行奇之多、所以表其權能也、種種

古　口　　固　
呆　亻　　保　恒　外　庶
皿　成　　盛　懷　暴　幾
皿　乃　　盈　恭　內　戰
　　　　　　順　愆　勝

力　且　　助
干　欠　　罕
頁　束　　賴　審　罰　重
也　亻　　他　判　犯　權
　　　　　　咸　廣　獨
　　　　　　己　援　任

亘　卜　　　　田　刂
裏　恭　　　　刂　已
小　入　　　　口　黃
頁　心　　　　乙　癸
十　　　　　　　　扌
共　　　　　　戍
川　夕　　　　丩　刂
　　日　　　　戈　四
　　門　　　　　　彳
　　衍　　　　彡　广
　　　　　　　　　扌
　　川　　　　产　里
　　　　　　　　　藋
　　戈　　　　月　蜀
　　　　　　　　　壬

　　人　　單　　千　彳
　　戈　　月　　木
　　夯　　　　　　犭
　　　　　　　　　　

牧

千雙字常

動偕新娶　香供酒邀　執油膏坐　流血憫號

力皆斤女　日共酉之　九由月土　疣皿閔虎
重亻亲取　禾亻氵敉　幸氵高从　氵ノ忄号

終臨

工役貧富　左右近交　餘論尤服　班旅盡招

父貝呂　エロ义　余侖艮　玨食皿召
千分山　ナ广斤六　言言月　リ方聿扌
　　　　食言月

語引之以譽耶穌也 廴音引雁音因
賽亞古之預言者也末期末日也九思君子之成德見論
右第九節記耶穌預言之確卽可信其無所不知矣賽以

發袁口裏　頁寸隹欠　卑襄心
广口士　公豈言其　亻言田
　　　　圭哥八雁　　　　　　行欠人心

廢園吉壞　頌對誰欺　街歌谷應　俾讓九思

示生睪　且系合辶
山女卩彳　亓子竹求

宗姓單微　祖孫答述　共獲濟進　誓乏哀哭
八獲齋辶　世廾氵隹　言之曰犬　折ノ衣卩

察貨度銀　赤白用給　提要發綱　合享永位
祭貝又民　亦曰卅合　是女殳岡　一口子水立
山化广金　一ノ門糸　扌西灬糸　人一口二亻

慧雨慈雲　震角播示　背架築壇　納匱載器
世勸
彗一茲雨　辰用番小　雨刀扌二　月木宣　內貴車叩
心雨心云　　　　　　　　　　　　　北加筑土　糸匚戈哭

音聶敦音僥

右第十節、記耶穌臨終之慘、皆所以救萬世之人也、福音

千雙字常

凡五百九十二字

淫淫祀也、叩音萱 敱音薇 戠音秩 戠音職
像而不變易夫風俗哉 簇也 匿耶和華之約匿 見舊約、
救萬世人自當心悅誠服、盡其分以待審判奈何崇事偶
像萬世人自當心悅誠服、盡其分以待審判奈何崇事偶
右第十一節記設教勸世之切言耶穌既已捨身爲人以

禺象可巳　　同戠口入　　同義叉谷
イイト冂　　金金厂十　　 𠆢戠皮𡈼
偶像阿囘　　銅鐵石木　　小言䌽イ
　　　　　　倉言石氵　　尙議變俗
　　　　　　創識破淫

昇與舉同、疑擬也、與尙書罪疑惟輕同義、

右第一節言耶穌升天之後萬事皆待之而鞫也凌騰也

辠咎疑輕　雪冤艱巨　覺昧醒迷　陰府抵拒

辛曰辛至　王兔艮　見未星辶　　會付氐巨
古厽矣車　雨山莫　　幽曰酉米　　卩广扌

待鞫
萬事啓穴屍甦　凌空升昇　寶座式憑　訟詞迫具

攵八死生　麥工廾丼　貝坐工心　公司之八
戶山尸更、　乂穴刀曰　鎤广弋馮　言言白目

第三章論人事

常字雙千編韻　字新法
　　　　　　　一名認

千雙字常

右第二節、言人當勤學以求正道也稽考求也

年幼　　孩嬰監孩　育誕元胎　饑泣乳急　席臥綿束

秉質清聰　概除雜慾　夙譖洪沾　盍早濯沐

兒輩謳誦　賦擇詩稽　齒牙申講　退邁均推

正道勤學　量才託授　衛翼扶持　詔戒誘誨　畫晚鑑茲

誇大縱放肆窘抑窘迫而屈抑也憾恨也機機變術權術

而求救也詭詐也駭驚也飾外為襲中藏為匿克能也伐

右第四節言人年齒既長習染漸深易墮惡途故當謹防

克伐驕縱　窘抑困窮　倘憾墮落　機術奚庸

｜戈喬從　　君卬木躬　　徜感土洛　　幾行大用
十亻馬糸　　穴扌口穴　　亻亻隋艹　　木木𥁕声

力　　　　斬士　　　　白木朱里　　危㐬衣兒
幺丶氵月　　羽冘歺立　　言言龍豸　　亥夭若衣
　　　　　　　　　　　　　　　　　　馬竹匚中

壯歲
幼丁漸壯　習染殊童　詭謙襲貌　駭笑匿衷

欲夙譴原罪也洪大也濯沐洗禮也　字所音垠
　　　　　　　　　　　　　　　夃音跋䚯音映乙古隱

右第三節言人初生之時惡孽未萌惟早當洗滌耳慾私

千雙字常

盡其職曰尸爵曠虛也祐福也
則永爲罪人矣嗜好也侮慢也愼篤誠篤之人也莅官不
右第五節讀書之人琴劍遨遊任情妄作苟不求慕正道
尸爵曠官　貪祐祀佛　哄唎囔朋　輪須鑒覆
業
士
博嗜簡篇．几筵勤讀　琴劍邂遊　專侮愼篤
庸用也 幺音邀乙音方卬抑古字

專耆間扁　延力寶　今引之之　寸每眞馬
十口竹竹　竹菫言　玨僉耑旂　虫亻十竹
肘廣曰　貝古已弗　法利賽月　兪頁金復
四日山　今亓亓亻　日日日月　車彡臣西
爪日山

工匠

操尺運斤　係誇傑步　弓矢皿料　精粗製鑄

枲 ㄏ昜 凸音薛
扌戶 夂 蘁音灌
亻軍 賣 䨻音繼
ㄣ 糸 旬音轟
亻言 卩
亻止 白
 　山

ㄑ
尸
亻言
亻止

系夸桀少　大斗　青且衣壽
　　　　　ㄧ米　米米製金

審判　則永爲罪人矣以水沃田曰灌植種也抹摸也寅敬惕鞠
右第六節農家者流三時辛苦希冀豐收苟不求慕正道

農田

泥塗奔走　竊認農耕　澤灌烟植　抹露踐塵

尼 氵涂 大十
土 卉 疋
疋 穴 禾忍 辰井
　 言 曲未
　
罒 蘁 因直
氵 火木

医 糸 厂
賣 足 山
豆 井
壽心 山 旬
相 面 革
田

一 危 文寸
足 虍 喆

末 路 戔土
扌 雨 足 鹿

千雙字常

右第八節 行商居買跋涉山川權營子母苟不求慕正道

音意八手 貝兌殳糸 戔萠思襄 主車弓倉
亻亻曲尚 工禾月敏 金氵虍才 馬广穴艹

倍億典掌 貢稅般繁 錢滿虜攘 駐庫穹蒼

巾出 貝買各岡 卩之嚴山 旦可工羊
山卩卜 四士山六 去印山鳥 土土氵

商客
市隅井際 買賣客商 却迎巖島 坦坷江洋

則永為罪人矣斤斧斤也泉刀錢也 梟音搖罭音瓖

右第七節工匠之儔鉤心鬪角作為奇巧苟不求慕正道

州直曷賞 水之 句吾木 之田匆卜
酉亻立亻 白𦣞 艹亻 車采走走

酬值竭償 泉刀還互 苟悟了休 連番趨赴

官服

卜賢徵哲、荷政輸忠、俘叛禦盜、驗印頒封

貝 數 口 何 夂 兪 心 孚 反 示 皿
毆 彳 折 艹 正 車 中 亻 半 御 冫
念 卩 頁 寸 馬 阝 分 圭

矣戚眷屬也昆玉兄弟也未裁同亦音洋隶音代

右第九節一室之內和氣致祥能如此者其孝友誠可嘉

刂 寸 聿 衣 粦 昔 叉 卑 日 言 民 原 隶 丁 儿 心
蒲 戶 攵 口 艹 十 女 女 雙 廿 木 氵 而 厶 尉
广 心 弓

刻薄肇衷、憐惜奴婢、普護根源、康寧允慰

力 戉 目 比 丶 亦 未 屯 子 耶 韃 十 弓 右 心
曰 王 女 女 糸 耂 父 丨 女 弓 亻 車

家居

嘉戚看承、昆玉姊妹、純孝爺懂、卑弱佑惠

則永為罪人矣卻退也迎進也坦平路坷險途音苛音透滿音門印音昂

千雙字常

義行

扁則壺大
亻亻卩酉
卩卩八

已襲戽土
土土山
阝阝

卩月斳泉
廾止鬥
止鬥卩

 無歲叟牛
艹禾亻
艹亻玄一

偏側陸奠

圯壞岸堅

那肯鬪隙

蕪穢侵牽

岡石辰岜
山般曰尸
曰尸

胡莫生辶
辶辶辶曰
曰毘

又叚樂辶
正古艹
古艹矣

而几盥目
雨食米扌
目扌

崗磐晨屆
職勾音葛
亻音胘

湖漢星遷

延蝦藥送

需飢糧捐

同徵龤同
皮音賢殳

小之躬自喻也、侯駕侯主之駕奏職、盡己之分、

矣卜枚卜徵聘也、賓幕中之客吏書役也、釁隙也貌躬貌

右第十節任君之事、鞠躬盡瘁能如此者其忠盡誠可嘉

八省山
史且敝
且卩艹

分古貌弓
酉鳥言
言艹身

矣馬天戠
亻加夹耳
亻耳

勾犬莧广
冒山山
厂山

賓吏阻薇

釁詰藐躬

侯駕奏職

曷厭寬宏

右第十二節此三等人能盡其分誠合於正道矣惟不求

犬岡黃惟　曰行才土　包艮冗侖　兄乖戔戒
戶糸木四　日曰門寒　扌忄氵　　八歹貝

戻綱橫羅　昌衢閉塞　抱恨沉淪　況兼殘賊

葷各山皿　言貝以赤　專艮朋死　馬見絲火
言忄宓明　與尚亻赤　車目山堇　敬者山里

謹恪密盟　譽賞似赫　轉眼崩毀　驚覩幽黑

勉
勸

不正也蕪汚也　由音塊　音六厈音漢臬同隙又音引

則壽可延需急也捐糧以急饑則荒可濟偏側物將壞而

嘉矣崗磐山之高者湖漢水之廣者嘏壽也送藥以却病、

右第十一節為善之人不存歧視能如此者其慈惠誠可

千雙字常

罪也、暮季末世也、濱水之涯也、崙山之巔也、進善退惡皆鯀必討其罪也、部黨類也、售甘甜言以誘人也、鳴鼓聲其

右第十三節今之邪黨橫行荼毒善類至末日之審判耶

嫁怨仗威　鳴鼓暮季　濱退崙逾　奈寡頂替
家心丈女　烏支日子　寶之倫之
女妃亻戍　口壹莫禾　氵民山俞　示百頁日
　　　　　　　　　　　　　　　大亼丁夫

偽
姦
邪黨毒蛇　卩黑母宅　領部吞噬　舌蜜售甘　燬虜倚勢
牙尚主虫　頁卩口筮　口虫口　　　　　毀男奇力
　　　　　令音天曰　千宀隹　　　　　火虍亻執

慕正道則不能自救其靈魂密盟盟之於心也赫顯赫也
橫罹無辜而蹈禍也沉淪陷溺也殘賊凶暴之人、密音伏

多 石 穌 艸
禾 麻 艹 虫
亡 鬼 昔
艹 艹 金 ノエ
然 登 火 目
火 火 昭 鼓

移 磨 蘇 蟲
燃 燈 照 瞥
忙 愧 錯 差
仰 慕 覲 附

方 舌 斐 室
戶 人 木 古
八 琶 主 伯
口 土 亻 宀
生 它 犬 豕
牛 馬 犭 豸
离 人 師 犬
人 門 犭 穴

房 舍 樓 臺
只 堪 佳 宿
牲 駝 狀 象
禽 閃 獅 突

王 丶 旦 下
犭 大 虍 粦
夂 詹 果 复
方 月 衣 月
ㄐ 心 古 辶

狂 犬 虐 鄰
剛 怨 姑 遜
放 膽 裸 腹
毛 髮 謗 刺

印 小 見 付
亻 莫 堇 下
反 主
木 木 土

板 柱 瓦 塔
僅 彰 樣 制
帶 繫 帕 懸
零 珍 表 飾

設 譬
己 自 主 無 預 替 者 也 壹 音 絎 百 古 百 字

堇 彡 叢 刂
亻 章 木 告
巾 糹 白 心
敞 巾 縣
令 彡 衣 巾
雨 王 主 自

千雙字常回

耶穌

嚴防假酵　_{厂段孝、叩阝酉}
暫辟慄杯　_{斬爵卄木、日辛栗不}
鷲鴿遁院　_{鬲鳥辶完、粥合盾口}
捕魚射圍　_{甫火寸韋、扌㐄身口}

翦枝撻打　_{羽支達丁、前木扌}
渴擬鹽充　_{曷疑盧儿、氵臥去}
腓骨慢折　_{非月曼斤、月皿卄}
寵壽旋增　_{龍疋會、人方土}

屢憶釘痛　_{尸卜金、裵意丁甬}
竟殲戈鋒　_{儿鐵ノ条、音万弋金}　_{糵音櫱參音蔘彡音衫艸音屮}
棘冠頭戴　_{束寸頁異、束完豆戈}
袍片搖紅　_{包工、衣片扌糸}

常回憶、屢憶釘痛狀、怪異也、蘇活也、竟殲戈鋒、無靈之物、不思得救也、塔高屋也、放縱也、裸露也、閃突形

右第十四節借譬以喻耶穌之道人人皆當遵行不可若

正道
傳宣

振枯拔草 扌木扌艹

吹籥也 鐵同簽𥬛音逢𥬗音出盧同鹽

遁避去也 射圖矢魚之戲 見春秋隱公傳 橄欖山名 吹管

之言行固在可堅信心也 被害而死日殉 腓骨脛骨也

右第十五節常憶耶穌受害之酷升天之榮而稽其生平

朔夏盤蹈 艹艹
核斗辨州 木扌
宥勇伸囚 宀甬亻口
苗糸齊魯 艹
品格呂歐

辰古戈旱 辰
有力申人
暨寒迄熱 既
曳杖緯球
田糸日 艹ノ 魚 口木口 叩各口 口欠 區欠

月夂皿䀎
𦫵般足 艹
亥十辛 木氵辛
旦冫辶火 既寒乞執
戈丈韋求 日木糸王

囊綻麻補 衣叩糸广
綻定林甫 叩糸
菓咒葉肥 艹艹艹 果几巴 月

索騎橄欖 糸奇敢覽 凸馬木木
到郇管吹 刂卩宀欠 至旬竹口

千雙字常

凡五百七十六字

也、㐅音撒

所向則鑒北斗以辨之緯象緯天之度也球地球地之體
修能文善武者也極北日朔中華日夏斗北夜行不知
改者也囚知罪而未伸也苗系猶苗裔也呂呂尙區歐區歐陽
寒暑不間固欲普救世人同享永福也振落也勇猛於悔
右第十六節此言傳道之教師伸說耶穌之道險阻不辭、

多也、冀望也、懺悔也、

以起下文也、迹迹象勳功勞楷模制之有定者也煩劇繁

右第一節鑒上主創造之迹以啓世人誠信之心承上章

楷模秘探　煩劇暢茂　始冀瞶聾　僉懺誤謬

皆葖必罙　頁　易戊　台異貴耳　从　鐵吳蓼
水木禾扌　火虍申艹　歹北目龍　△叩卜言言

昌
緬迹溯勳　儘鮮缺漏　擲畍某儔　搴裳叄叩
總
面辶朔力　盍羊夫雨　鄭刀木壽　手衣叄卜
糸亦氵熏　亻魚岳汙　扌田甘亻　寒尙厽口

第四章論儔類

常字雙千編韻　字新法
　　　　　　　一名認

千雙字常

地理
       夂九
牧   ㄅ穴裂
究   ㄇ山品
寰   ㄈ
區

爲旱多雨而災爲潦變和變調調理
氣也綠繞廻環也迅疾也久晴日暘久雨日霢不雨而災
右第二節就天之可見者以驗上主之功有如此嵐天之

長短闊狹　　豆活夾
　　　　　　矢門犭
凸凹崎嶇　　　奇區
　　　　　　　山山
函燕崖峽　　　豕豕
　　　　　　　山山
　　　　　　　山厎夾

　　之田田音　孔音信雀音窺炊開去
迅雷奮響　　孔雨雀鄉
疏霜催凋　　荒相崔周　易淫干潦
暘霢旱潦　　疋雨亻　　日雨曰氵
　　　　　　　　　　　立賣言
苧覲變調　　宁見炊又周
　　　　　　立賣言

天文
晴嵐繚繞　　青風尞堯　　　　
　　　　　　日山糸糸
瞻矖層霄　　詹屬會肖
　　　　　　目目尸雨
霞輝林豔　　叚軍木盍
　　　　　　雨光木豐
霓彩渡消　　兒彡度肖
　　　　　　雨采氵

　　　　　　　令
　　　　　　　時
悅　併　盪　蠻　辯　也　究　有　　　爭　靑　靜　　　訟　火　熾　　　戠　王　璣　　　心　匆　怨
歧　程　疆　貊　辰　塹　察　第　　　口　卜　占　　　炎　各　燄　　　行　奐　衡　　　之　虞　遽
徑　塹　拓　包　訝　坑　也　三　　　安　日　晏　　　樂　火　爍　　　僉　馬　驗　　　著　足　躇
抄　劃　輿　刮　午　也　寰　節　　　堯　日　曉　　　花　石　硫　　　目　竹　算　　　壽　足　躊
　　　　　　　　　江　區　就
　　　　　　　　　爲　四　地
　　　　　　　　　天　海　之
　　　　　　　　　塹　之　廣
　　　　　　　　　　　內　大
　　　　　　　　　　　高　者
　　　　　　　　　　　出　以
　　　　　　　　　　　爲　驗
　　　　　　　　　　　凸　上
　　　　　　　　　　　低　圭
　　　　　　　　　　　下　之
　　　　　　　　　　　爲　功
　　　　　　　　　　　凹　有
　　　　　　　　　　　崎　如
　　　　　　　　　　　嶇　此
　　　　　　　　　　　路　歟
　　　　　　　　　　　不　考
　　　　　　　　　　　平　同

千雙字常

右第五節、山川之奇幻具見匠心人當推上主之功能勿

章卒非累　朝由史冀　么丁弓秦　圭元攵奇
山羽扌虫　氵共馬馬　工么工至　亻王亻山

嶂翠排螺　潮黃駛驥　玄幻巧臻　佳玩攸寄

山
代山山山　冐氵之　鐫卜爪氵　步步手齊
山獄欽疑　冐氵召尼　鐫卜爪氵　步步㐱足

水
山
岱嶽嶔嶷　渭川迢遞　鑒險覓津　陟涉攀躋

躇躊猶豫不決之貌 氵音衫戠音熾虞音據

時過之速也璣衡璇璣玉衡所以占測者也怱遽促迫也

怱促而急求永福也雙九日月也蹢躅行貌熾燄爍硫喻

右第四節、時序運行不息少縱卽歷春秋人宜知光陰之

非人之所能測也、倜儻卓立也、遴選也、薦進也、順人而阿
右第六節、上主生人、靈蠢不一、而締造之苦心實有奧妙、

人品

髫儂耆耉

顝頋伶俐

召童曰口

頁頁令利

兩干亻亻

要析胃毛

糸曰虍亐

月月酉糸

包丕巳帝

少大頁堯

女白皮食

婁晰膚毫

胞胚配締

妙奧頗饒

周黨夾豕

亻亻亻亐

辶鷹力大

彝艹厲將

昏敖幾朝

言亻言口

倜儻俠豪

遴薦勵獎

謟傲謨喇

如螺也駛驥潮來迅急如驥之駛也、臻至也、字幺音邀
麃音斯毅鉴本

水名迢遞遼闊也登山曰陟、履水曰涉、排螺言諸山排列

徒羨佳玩之寄也、岱嶽泰山名山之宗也、歁嶷聳立貌渭

千雙字常

右第七節宮室華美承門祐者猶恥玷汙人奈何不求心
之清潔哉複重也聯縣連接不斷也輻輳聚集也衍延也

小土予羊　禾寸則既　行癸之休　心占眉冓
齋埶广厂　而壴皆从市　氵庠牙厂　耳王木木

齋塾序庠　廩廚廁廄　衍慶迤庥　恥玷楣構

一射隹即　复皆从市　文監絲系　奇囱昌奏
田木周广　衣土大⺤戶　非木耳帛　糸穴車車

宮室
畫榭雕廊　複堦夾牖　斐檻聯縣　綺窗輻輳

分也締造也饒多也　鷹音荐萹音門
笑人曰嘲顢頇千言愚蠢之人辦事無眉目也縷細絲也晰
附之曰諂凌人而蔑視之曰傲微諷以刺人曰譏曲言以

器用

歕 瓜 平 才
西 角 言 木
　　昔 貝 左 甫
　　亻次 亻車
覂 舥 評 材
裝潢而不急在內之寶貴乎、
借 資 佐 輔
簪音驂羉音瓊皷音激
睡 眠 榻 牀
　　垂 民 豻 木
　　目 目 日 爿
　　木 夕 竹
饔 飧 匕 筯

服飾

葛 裘 綌 紛
衒 耀 襟 袖
右第八節、服飾僅美外觀敉靈必享永福亦奚戀在外之
掩 映 副 鑲
耆 齡 限 促
邅 戀 裝 潢
爓 爛 輝 煌

迃迎也、庥吉祥也、玷汚也、楣門楣搆堂搆、燹音愛、燮音伏、綹音關

千雙字常

林郎虎久 王王王 馬留武夫 爭榮崔縈 山山王王 𦉯乃令女 呈子口吳

琳瑯琥玖 王王王 石石石 碼碯碔砆 石石石 岬嶸璀璨 轀孕舍娛

寶珍
寸珠咫璧 朱貝玉 王尺辟 青珩丹瑚 王 行胡 洛鐘泗磬 各童四石 氵金 秦鼎唐鑪 禾 廣金

也、哉、驟驂也、軛器之有棱者也、塵、拂塵也、楮紙也、鑪署次序右第九節人造器物以適己用何不修德爲上主之重器

揮塵挽韁 軍主兔韁 扌鹿扌革 吮筆裁楮 允聿衣者 曰 戈木 女寧慧諸 爪貝禾亻 妥貯穩儲 父牛虗者 爪 舟亻月四 般件鑪署

右第十一節、五音迭奏、宮商克諧、不知樂者、不能和聲也、

嵓敷峯又延車也手貝永羽皆監于世則

汫山回雨車雨制庚言合言泣竹音泣

口个單糸之員堅將林令衣巾泣金列白

湍激峯廻 霆轟電擊 虜詠翕諧

虛 竹彈絲 蕭韶捌拍 逸韻鏗鏘 淋鈴裂帛

音樂 嘘 音錄顯音溫 濫竽羞測

石也崢嶸高峻貌璀璨玉光也韞藏也 殷音聲廖音聊糸

泗磬石磬之能浮者琳瑯琥玖美玉之名碼砆砆砆皆寶

人心含孕韞藏伺其永寶八寸曰咫洛鐘銅鐘之寶貴者

右第十節、珍奇之物、猶聖道也、珍奇秘於庫藏、聖道寓於

千雙字常

右第十二節花木秀於一時，上主猶畀以景色眾人生於

兆子兇愛　公百寸、　　　參　　妃有甘虫
木木垃日　木木而冬　走仁工酉曰　艹口酉鬲

桃李競暖　　松栢耐冬　　趁候釀景　　苑囿酣融

旦开分眉　乃鹿而重　黑民易卯　泉陰吾同
月女米女　禾丽山金　代氵木木　糸艹木木

花木
脂妍粉媚　　秀麗崇鍾　　黛痕楊柳　　綠蔭梧桐

不能吹者也　夆音逢

之疾峯廻山勢之紆譬樂聲之徐速也濫竽有竽之名而
拊撫同鏗鏘樂之節奏淋鈴曲名裂帛樂聲也湍激水流
聖教廣播遠近交孚不知道者不能行善也簫韶古樂名

種也、腥羶鳥獸之肉、音音透叕音輟 冰同水乂古五字

滅罪而救靈不必妄拜他神尙偶像之多飫饜足也、藝

更求腥羶徒侈肴饌之盛猶之聖教爲古今之正道足以

右第十三節蔬菜爲天地之正味足以衞生而悅口不必

叕 顏乏分 扌 斂

且爵爾夫 月次星宣 巽有多水 食乂亻泰

包夫方香 執田夂畜采 刂采微 火癸合介

掇擷鬱芬 咀嚼彌快 胡荽腥羶 饌肴侈泰

食食艹殷 扌扌懋艹 古羊月羊 食乂亻泰

蔬菜

鮑飫芳馨 藝畝蓄菜 剖瓜採薇 煮葵拾芥

一世上主更望其復新酣暢也 酣古龍字兇同昆

千雙字常

鱗介

鱗介蕃滋

鱗 粦 一番茲
魚 个 卄 氵

譜題蠱磋

龜鼈黿鼉

鯤鰲鯨鱷

普頁鹿崔
言是鹿石

跙跙跙
敝元盥

昆魚京曇
魚敖魚
魚魚

也 蠢 俗騰字粵音緬勇敷古文

衣食之不足而徒烹庖之為亟哉蓊飛也遨遊也敷豫足
右第十四節鳥獸之微上主猶備饎餌以養其生人何憂

鳥獸

騰祥毓瑞 鳳蓊麟遨 驊騮馳騁 鸞鶴翔翱

鸑 羊充巾 鳥羽羰辶 華留也粵 鳥鳥羽羽
月示每王 凡者鹿敖 馬馬馬馬 崔崔羊皋

雞塒豚柵 鴻渚鵲巢 饎餌敷豫 詎亟烹庖

隹時豖冊 鳥者鳥果 羞耳攵象 巨二火包
奚土月木 江氵昔巛 食食勇予 言又亨广

隹時豕冊
奚土月水

鳥者鳥果
江氵昔巛

羞耳攵象
食食勇予

言句亨广

蟲
昆蠶織蛛組
　　　蚓唱蟬吟
　　　徜徉遂閣
　　　紬繹開庭

蜘戠朱且
虵絲虫糸
虫口虫口
引昌單今
彳彳山門
由罨月廷
糸糸門广

入大水為蛤見禮記月令俄頃少頃也鬆音顯
靈哉蕃滋言粄多也淬泗沒水之貌蝗落水則化蝦又雀
頃耳可見人生甚為貴重奈何竟等於鱗介而不思救其
右第十五節鱗介之族雖多然中無靈魂其跳躍不過少

淬蝗掬蝦　泗雀撈蛤　卵濕累摰　俄頃跳躍
氵皇扌叚　氵雀扌合　卵縣糸子　我頁兆翟
卒皇射段　泗小扌虫　八氵田茲　彳七足足
氵虫扌虫　因雀勞合

千雙字常

絲預
力閒催
匴勉肅雍　荒之傷且
免中歺　　十夆歺歺
　　　　　慌逢殤姐　區殳乙牛
　　　　　　　　　　身殼非山　月心炙疋
　　　　　　　　　軀殼匪牢　　　　　　生匚酉林
　　　　　　　　　　　　　　　肯歷酸楚

閒也、么麼渺小也、忖思也、凄凄辛艱辛、
得免淒楚也、組亦織也、孿肉屑也、蟻攢肉屑有如獵然鬪
艱辛之事人則生命甚重失救甚苦其當如何信心而始
右第十六節么麼小蟲暫有生命所以絕無思慮不知有

　　　　力肉鼠義　　專反共匴　　ム么舜分　　芒寸妻十
拋孿獵蟻　扌絲犭虫　　扌食鬪虫　　ノ麻目目　　門忄亠立　搏飯鬪蠅　　么麼瞬盼　　岡忖淒辛
　　　　　　　　　　　　　　　　鼠音獵
　　　　　　　　　　　　　　　　兢音華 蚰音昆

引規告湯、宣大䜣、曰亦自窌

矢穴氵艹、曰亦自窌、糸匕氵禾、堯目金彥

紉窺浩蕩、喧奕无邊、緝熙淵穆、翹睎鈞顏

羽弟勺頁

恐懼之貌 鬭淵古文

順天死日殤壽死日殂軀殼肉身也肯小罪慝隱惡悚惶

惕臭腐之期靈魂之失於救耳黽勉勤求也肅誠敬雍和

而知肉體之不牢罪惡之未免邀結同志恐懼所求蓋深

右第十七節言人當勤求於道致敬盡禮畏死亡之日近

弟屍束呈 頁手羋呂 一丰日取

氵辰 束呈 步扨亻 日吳 勺言 言易犬肉 敬亻自府

涕淚悚惶 頻挈伴侶 旦肄旬諏 警惕臭腐

千字雙常

柬 刀 糸 橑　　易 兀 艸　　咸見申需　　中文乙皿
主 亻　　　　氵 垚 亚　　亻夫糸亻　　亻門子子

策絜臣僚　　禹湯堯舜　　箴規紳儒　　仲閔孔孟

紺參同穆

除也傴僂鞠躬也踧踖恭敬也冥頑不靈者也悛改也
奕宣著盛大之貌緝熙光明也淵穆深遠之意懟怨也
謹恭順感受聖靈自改其前日之冥頑矣浩蕩廣大貌喧
當沉思邈慮若或見之則跪拜禱祝化其不善之心而敬
右第十八節上主之德廣大無名上主之功光明可見人

甫 先 心心月丿　　　　　區娿叔昔
勹勹足足　斬對疋冊　　　亻亻足足

俛甸跊跙　　懟懟胥剛　　　傴僂踧踖
　　　　　　　　　　　　　　　　　　大頁余叕
　　　　　　　　　　　　　　　　　門月元亻十
　　　　　　　　　　　　　　　冥頑徐悛

四章統計二千十六字

凡六百八字

浮華曰奢樸實曰淳甄別也膺心胃之間、

豈怖永火之無救始盡心以昭事上帝哉策勉也絜領也

當斟酌於眞僞之途甄別其信從之準以循當然之則而

右第十九節言耶穌之道其教人致君澤民正心誠意人

斗勺者享　又旡票十　火人布毯　無月攵民心
徒西大氵　雗亞木淮　火八十火　寸雇每豸
斟酌奢淳　雙甄標準　炎火怖燒　撫膺敏懇

TABLE OF ELEMENTS. 131

From this table all those characters are excluded, which are found either in the text or among the radicals. Many of those contained in the list are obsolete, except as *elements*. The imperfect elements have no fixed sounds, but a Chinese teacher will find no difficulty in giving them names.

CHAPTER I.

Ts'ung, Same as 從 from.

Yüih, To cut off the feet.

Tso, Ancient form of 左。

Yuen, A Small worm.

Cha, Just now, anon.

Pih, A prince.

Ü, A kind of ape.

Wu, Ancient form of 五。

Lü, To draw with the hand.

Ling, Same as 靈。

Fu, A sorcerer.

Ch'u, Same as 處。

Fuh, Same as 復。

We, Stomach.

Chau, Seek, pay balance.

Ko, An individual.

Tah, Virtue 德。

Yai, Impede.

Yih, Original.

Shah, for 煞 baleful.

I, Tranquil.

S, A monastery.

Ch'uh, Step of the left foot.

Tiau, Suspend, sympathize. 弔。

Cheu, A broom.

Tue, Heap.

Shuh, Father's younger brother.

P'ih, Equal, fellow.

Sah, Thirty.

Fuh, High, thick,

Kiang, Descend, 降。

Kwan, String together, string of cash.

Lün, Narrate.

Pih, Shovel.

T'un, The buttocks.

Cheu, Helmet.

Shoh, A spoon.

Leu, Name of a star.

132 ANALYTICAL READER.

豐 Li, A sacrificial vessel.
刁 Tiau, A kind of kettle drum.

酉 Ts'iu, To ferment wine.
昷 Wen, Kindness.

IMPERFECT ELEMENTS.

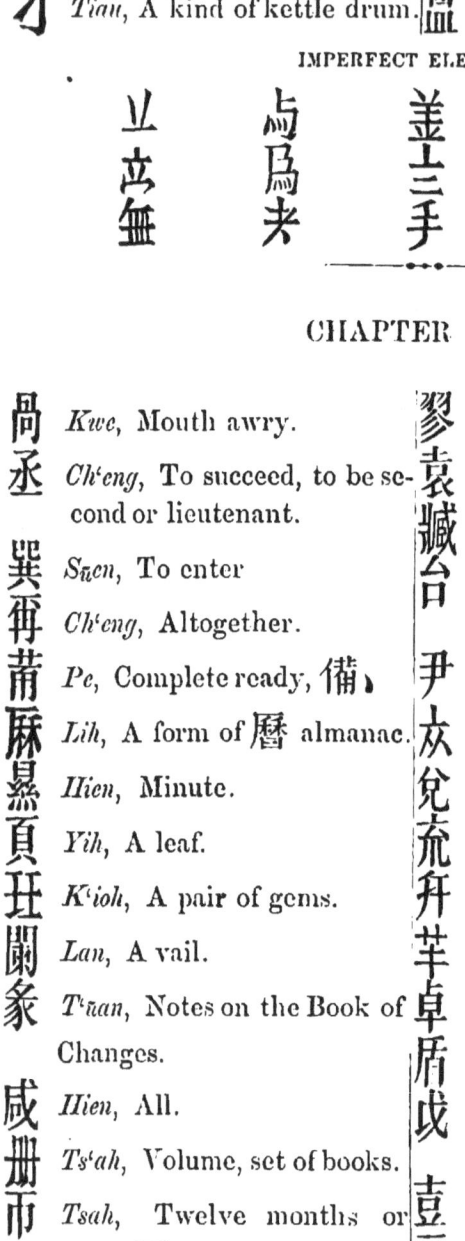

CHAPTER II.

咼 Kwe, Mouth awry.
丞 Ch'eng, To succeed, to be second or lieutenant.
巽 Suen, To enter.
冉 Ch'eng, Altogether.
莆 Pe, Complete ready, 備.
厤 Lih, A form of 曆 almanac.
纍 Hien, Minute.
頁 Yih, A leaf.
玨 K'ioh, A pair of gems.
關 Lan, A vail.
象 T'uan, Notes on the Book of Changes.
咸 Hien, All.
册 Ts'ah, Volume, set of books.
市 Tsah, Twelve months or years' 匝.

叅 Luh, Fly high.
袁 Yüen, Family name.
臧 Tsang, Virtuous, prosperous.
台 T'ai, Term of respect, form of 臺.
尹 Ing, Mayor.
灰 Yih, 亦 Also.
兌 Tüe, Exchange.
㐬 Liu, A tassel, for 旒.
开 Kien, Equal.
芉 Yang, Sheep, goat, for 羊.
卓 Choh, Firm, stable, eminent.
厈 Tun, Shield.
戉 Yüih, Fasces, emblems of power.
壴 Chu, Display of music.
亘 Keng, Continuous, perpetual.

TABLE OF ELEMENTS.

Ki, Successive, 繼)
Süe, Name of a place.
Ch', Simple, stupid.
Pi, Close, narrow, for 鄙)
Fuh, Govern, order.
Yü, Yes, a girl's answer.
K'ien, A fragment.
Kwai, To differ, distorted.
Lu, A vessel.
Hwan, A small bird.
Ts'ung, Quick of hearing, intelligent.
Kih, for 擊 to attack.
Nih, for 逆 to oppose.
Chüen, To walk slowly.
Yang, Middle, invite.
Yau, To dip water.
Ch'uan, Pierce through, string together.
Yin, A quarrel between dogs.
Kiung, Open windows.
P'ien, Flat. 匾)
Ch'ih, Command.
Mau, The 4th hour.
Hiuh, Cattle, for 畜)
Kü, An eagle glance.

Nu, Slave.
Lüan, Disorder, for 亂)
K'ü, Implacable strife.
K'iu, A hillock.
T'un, Store up, accumulate.
Hai, The 12th hour.
Yih, Espionage.
Ling, Besides, other.
P'ai, flow apart, appoint 派)
T'o, sue, Fall, name of a dynasty.
Ch', A goblin, for 離)
Long, A title.
Yang, For 陽) the bright or male principle.
Tsan, Praise, associate.
Yung, A covered way.
King, Straight waves.
Ts'an, A particle.
Chüe, wan, Grassy.
Ts, Able, sustain.
Hüen, A kind of furnace.
T'au, Pottery.
Yü, A moment.
Ts'ih, Concubine.
Ku, To hire.

丙 *Ping*, The 3rd of the 10 stems.

丂 *Yü*, For 于,

威 *Mih*, Consume, destroy.

討 *T'au*, Beg, assail.

蜀 *Chuh*, A name of Szechuen.

壬 *Jin*, 9th of the 10 stems.

呆 *Yai*, Stupid.

褱 *Hwai*, Bosom.

券 *Hüen*, A document.

冉 *Jan*, A name.

襄 *Siang*, Assist, praise.

圭 *Kwe*, A badge of office, a baton.

敫 *Kiau*, A stream of light, music.

雁 *Ing*, A kind of bird.

号 *Hau*, Sign, cry, for 號,

虎 *Hu*, Tiger.

筑 *Chuh*, To build.

亶 *T'an*, T'an-fu, a name.

吅 *Hüen*, A cry, noise, for 喧,

岡 *Kang*, A hill, for 崗,

敫 *Cheng*, To test, for 徵,

尢 *Chuh*, A medecine.

戠 *T'i*, Name of a place.

倉 *Ts'ang*, Granary.

譜 *An*, Understand.

巠 *Ying*, To beg.

彗 *Hwe*, A comet.

IMPERFECT ELEMENTS.

曲 斤 皀 皂 业 豕 氏 囱 厶 夕 囪 冗 寒 業 飠 灬 尹 ○ ○ ○

CHAPTER III. 135

麥窰馮会

Ling, A tomb for 陵﹚
Pau, Precious for 寶﹚
Fung, A name.
Yin, The female principle, for 陰﹚
Kih, The root of a tree.
Keu, Mutual gains.
Tuan, A section, ball.
Ing, Necklace.
Fu, Faith.
Fuh, Luxuriant.
Tih, A kind of pheasant.
Chan, To cut off.
Wan, Flowing tears.
Chu, Scarlet.
We, High, perilous.
Mau, for 貌﹚
K'iau, Lofty.
Kan, Feel, move.
Fu, Diffuse, for 敷﹚
King, An herb.
Chüan, Special, for 專﹚
I, By, for 以﹚
T'u, Road, a name.
Hwe, Flowers.

Ts'ien, Minute.
Kiu, A vine.
Hung, Loud noise.
Kw'a, Great.
Kih, Oppressive.
Kü, Sentence, clause.
Ts'u, Grass.
Man, Equal.
Shuh, A small bean.
Meu, 5th of the 10 stems.
Ts, To stop.
P'u, Abundant.
Ling,, Ignis fatuus.
Ch, Single, a classifier.
We, Soothe, comfort.
Yü, Royal, drive a chariot.
Pi, Spoiled.
Kai, Beg.
Hien, Spinach.
Kung, Arms, for 肱﹚
Choh, To cut down.
Sien, Ascend high.
Siau, To long, for 笑﹚
Yuen, Small insect.
Loh, Lump of earth 陸﹚

An, Shore, 岸)
Hih, Hole in a wall.
Meu, Lowing of a cow.
Jung, Hurried.
Jung, A weapon.
Ts'ien, A bamboo tally.
Fung, To drag an ox.
Yien, Salt, for 鹽)
Man, Long.
Lih, Tremble.
Chuh, Soft boiled rice.
Wan, Finish.
Fu, Just now.
Lan, See, read.
T'o, Snake for 牠)
Sh, Grass used in divination.

T'eu To spit.
Tsau, A flea, also for 早 early.
Nien, Twenty.
Yän, A bird faithful to its mate.
Chang, 10 ft, Chinese 141 in, English.
Snih, 11th hour.
Yang, A long stream.
Hien A district.
Cheng, Long black hair, for 鬢)
Chan, Garrulous.
Pah, Running of a dog.
P'ang, The side.
Peh, 100, A centurion.
K'ih, Beg.

IMPERFECT ELEMENTS.

CHAPTER IV. 137

面 *Mien*, Face.

熏 *Hun*, A flame.

夬 *Kuih*, Different, certain.

鄭 *Cheng*, Dignity, name of a kingdom.

吳 *Wu*, A name.

憭 *Liau*, Bright, clear.

肖 *Siau*, Like, good.

崔 *Ch'ue*, Lofty.

宁 *Chu*, A vestibule.

厓 *Yai*, Shore.

呈 *Ch'eng*, Hand up.

哉 *Chih*, Not explained by K'ang-hi.

匆 *Ts'ung*, Haste, for 怱.

欽 *K'ing*, Respect, imperial.

虎 *S*, A horned tiger.

鑿 *Chuh*, Chisel, for 鑿.

樊 *Fan*, A fence, lattice.

考 *K'au*, Investigate.

廌 *Hiai*, A one horned goat.

敖 *Au*, Ramble for 遨.

析 *Sih*, Separate.

丕 *P'e*, Great.

綵 *Kwan*, Weave.

眉 *Me*, Eyebrow.

餐 *Ts'an*, A meal.

奄 *Yien*, Detain, conceal.

昜 *T'ah*, Buoyant.

畺 *Kiang*, Boundary, for 疆.

彔 *Luh*, Wood carving.

員 *Yuen*, Round, dollar, officer.

堅 *Kien*, Firm.

廷 *T'ing*, Palace.

庚 *Keng*, 7th of the stems.

丑 *Ch'eu*, 2nd hour.

癸 *Kwe*, 10th of the stems.

丽 *Li*, Beautiful, for 麗.

叕 *Chueh*, Join.

頡 *Kih*, Neck erect.

甹 *P'ing*, Rapid utterance.

崔 *Hoh*, Crane.

皇 *Kau*, Call, high, a name.

旉 *Fu*, Diffuse, for 敷.

亨 *Heng*, Good luck.

余 *She*, A family name.

噩 *Oh*, Fright.

匊 *Kuh*, Handful, for 掬.

鼠 *Lih*, Hairy.

芒 *Mang*, Beard of grain.
壳 *K'uh*, Shell, for 殼)
規 *Kwe*, A rule.
耳 *Ts'ih*, Satire.
兔 *Ts'an*, A hare.

开 *Yuen*, Abyss, for 淵)
勻 *Yuing*, Equal, for 均)
彥 *Yien*, Virtuous, Excellent.
忌 *Ki*, Envy, hate.

IMPERFECT ELEMENTS.

獄　囟　声　甲
了　凩　由　○

STYLES OF WRITING.

Seal, Old Official, Grass, Business, Pattern.

未生民來 前有上帝 惟一真神 無聖能比
六日力作 先闢天地 萬物多焉 既希且異
未生民來 前有上帝 惟一真神 無聖能比
六日力作 先闢天地 萬物多焉 既希且異
未生民來 先闢天地 惟一真神 既希且異
六日力作 前有上帝 萬物多焉 無聖能比
未生民來 先闢天地 惟一真神 既希且異

Seal, Grass, Business.

來生民來　前有上帝　惟一真神　無聖能比
六曰力作　先闢天地　萬物多焉　既希且異
遂亦和土　將為靈矣　命雲賜基　千百皆興
後使宜家　乃父使事　設立曰友　爾家如自
兄弟承志　母不立亭　發眼善惡　勿強手民
告云可信　武當兄平　閱三摩會　乃死固此
中傳亞伯　羊祭陪延　喬子耆尼　融穀反今
已殺彼妹　但肉彩名　壽身辰尼　彫馬羅金
之意非答　其儀已吧　郎由是時　木水四行

STYLES OF WRITING. 141

Seal, Grass, Business.

卷撒全死 何問儕羣
居八泥七 各拉入門
俾八耶穌 彼賓穌主
兼率至殿 左會叓出
歎禮穿湳 司十貴徒
楷者國也 由弓山矛

第歸方蓋 則同義人
故又督教 甚加世福
勞間于弓 倫生捄為
扣約雲玉 必知強形
冷迦城弓 巳米鎧踦
王丙濕雛 復章暗譎

常字雙千釋義

A

VOCABULARY

OF

TWO THOUSAND FREQUENT CHARACTERS

WITH

THEIR MOST COMMON SIGNIFICATIONS,

AND

THE SOUNDS OF THE PEKING DIALECT.

Note.

For the sake of brevity, those significations which are most easily deducible, have been omitted; and the student is expected to bear in mind that feature of the language which admits of the same *word* being employed without alteration in different parts of speech. Thus after giving 生 as *life* it would be superfluous to define it further as to *live, alive*, &c.

The alphabet of Mr. Edkins, to whom I am indebted for the Peking sounds, differs a little from that employed in the preceding parts of this book—for example. *i* is used to express a sibillation, and *è* has the sound of *e* in there.

The following table taken from Mr. Edkins' Progressive Lessons, will furnish an index to his use of the tone marks.

First tone	上平	shang p'ing	烏 ,wu
Second tone	上聲	shang sheng	五 'wu
Third tone	去聲	c'hü sheng	務 wu'
Fourth tone	入聲	juh sheng	屋 wuh
Fifth tone	下平	hia p'ing	無 .wu or wu

THE 214 RADICALS.

WITH THEIR

SOUNDS AND SIGNIFICATIONS.

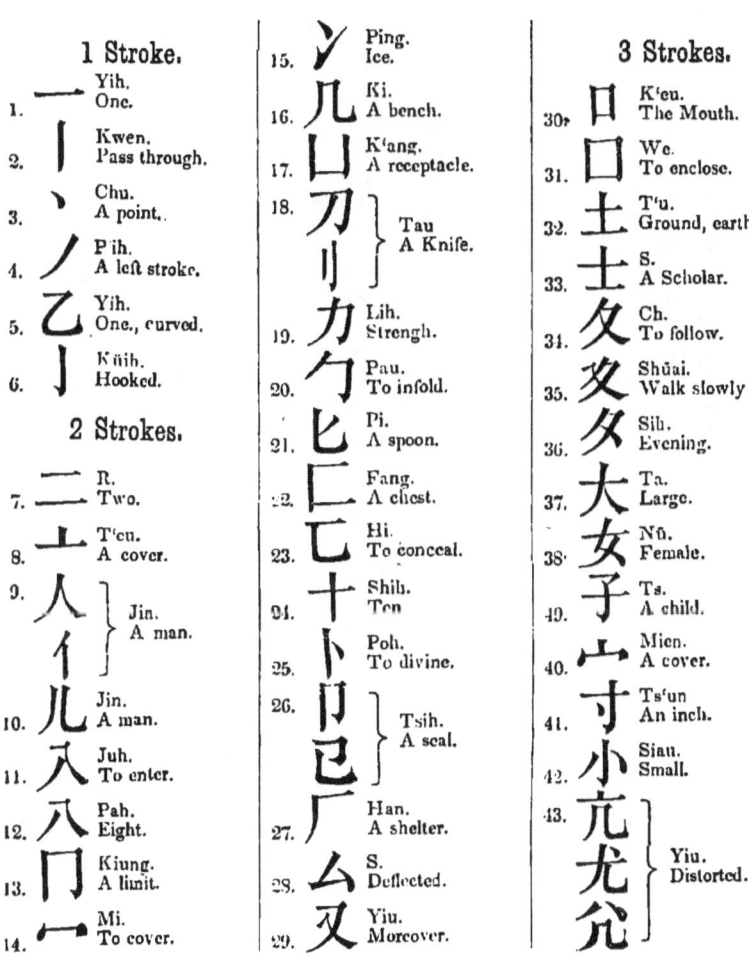

1 Stroke.

1. Yih. One.
2. Kwen. Pass through.
3. Chu. A point.
4. P'ih. A left stroke.
5. Yih. One, curved.
6. Küh. Hooked.

2 Strokes.

7. R. Two.
8. T'eu. A cover.
9. Jin. A man.
10. Jin. A man.
11. Juh. To enter.
12. Pah. Eight.
13. Kiung. A limit.
14. Mi. To cover.
15. Ping. Ice.
16. Ki. A bench.
17. K'ang. A receptacle.
18. Tau. A Knife.
19. Lih. Strength.
20. Pau. To infold.
21. Pi. A spoon.
22. Fang. A chest.
23. Hi. To conceal.
24. Shih. Ten.
25. Poh. To divine.
26. Tsih. A seal.
27. Han. A shelter.
28. S. Deflected.
29. Yiu. Moreover.

3 Strokes.

30. K'eu. The Mouth.
31. We. To enclose.
32. T'u. Ground, earth.
33. S. A Scholar.
34. Ch. To follow.
35. Shŭai. Walk slowly.
36. Sih. Evening.
37. Ta. Large.
38. Nü. Female.
39. Ts. A child.
40. Mien. A cover.
41. Ts'un. An inch.
42. Siau. Small.
43. Yiu. Distorted.

ANALYTICAL READER.

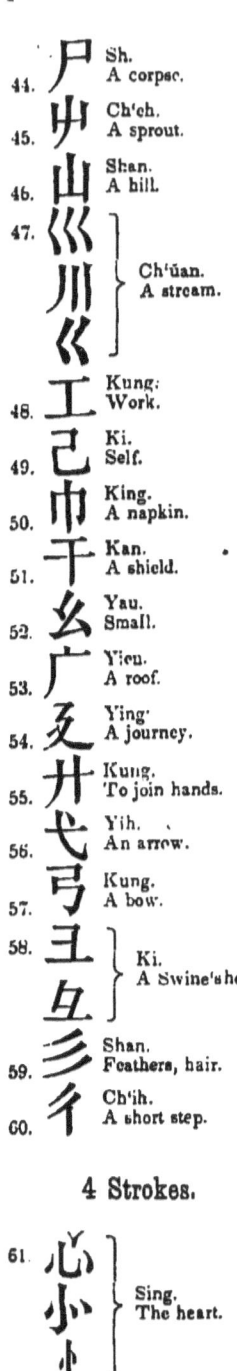

#	Char	Romanization	Meaning
44.	尸	Sh.	A corpse.
45.	屮	Ch'ch.	A sprout.
46.	山	Shan.	A hill.
47.	巛 川 巜	Ch'üan.	A stream.
48.	工	Kung.	Work.
49.	己	Ki.	Self.
50.	巾	King.	A napkin.
51.	干	Kan.	A shield.
52.	幺	Yau.	Small.
53.	广	Yien.	A roof.
54.	廴	Ying.	A journey.
55.	廾	Kung.	To join hands.
56.	弋	Yih.	An arrow.
57.	弓	Kung.	A bow.
58.	彐 彑	Ki.	A Swine's head.
59.	彡	Shan.	Feathers, hair.
60.	彳	Ch'ih.	A short step.

4 Strokes.

#	Char	Romanization	Meaning
61.	心 忄	Sing.	The heart.
62.	戈	Ko.	A spear.
63.	戶	Hu.	A door.
64.	手 扌	Sheu.	A hand.
65.	支	Ch.	A branch.
66.	攴 攵	P'ah.	A blow.
67.	文	Wen.	Literature.
68.	斗	Teu.	A measure.
69.	斤	King.	A catty, a pound.
70.	方	Fang.	A Square.
71.	无	Wu.	Without.
72.	日	Jih.	The sun, a day.
73.	曰	Yüih.	To speak.
74.	月	Yüih.	The moon.
75.	木	Muh.	Wood, timber.
76.	欠	K'ien.	To owe.
77.	止	Ch.	To stop.
78.	歹 歺	Tai.	Evil.
79.	殳	Ch'u.	Weapons.
80.	毋	Wu.	Do not.
81.	比	Pi.	To compare.
82.	毛	Mau.	Hair.
83.	氏	Sh.	The family name.
84.	气	K'i.	Breath.
85.	水 氵	Shŭe.	Water.
86.	火 灬	Ho.	Fire.
87.	爪 爫	Chau.	Claws.
88.	父	Fu.	Father.
89.	爻	Hiau.	To imitate.
90.	爿	Ch'uang.	A bed.
91.	片	P'ien.	A splinter.
92.	牙	Ya.	Teeth.
93.	牛	Niu.	A cow.
94.	犬 犭	K'üin.	A dog.

5 Strokes.

#	Char	Romanization	Meaning
95.	玄	Huin.	Dark, sombre.
96.	玉 王	Yuh.	A gem.
97.	瓜	Kwa.	A melon.
98.	瓦	Wa.	A tile.
99.	甘	Kan.	Sweet.

TABLE OF RADICALS.

#	Char	Reading	Meaning
100.	生	Sheng.	Life.
101.	用	Yung.	To use.
102.	田	T'ien.	A field.
103.	疋	P'ih.	A piece of cloth.
104.	疒	Nih.	Sick.
105.	癶	Poh.	To separate.
106.	白	Peh.	White.
107.	皮	P'i.	Skin.
108.	皿	Ming.	A vessel.
109.	目 四	Muh.	The eyes.
110.	矛	Meu.	A spear.
111.	矢	Sh.	An arrow.
112.	石	Shih.	A stone.
113.	示 礻	Sh.	To show.
114.	禸	Jeu.	To creep.
115.	禾	Ho.	Growing, rice.
116.	穴	Hüih.	A cave.
117.	立	Lih.	To stand.

6 Strokes.

#	Char	Reading	Meaning
118.	竹	Chuh.	Bamboo.
119.	米	Mi.	Hulled rice.
120.	糸	S.	Silk.
121.	缶	Feu.	Earthenware.
122.	网 冈 皿 冗	Wang.	A net.
123.	羊	Yang.	A sheep.
124.	羽	Yŭ.	Wings.
125.	老	Lau.	Aged.
126.	而	R.	And, still.
127.	耒	Le.	A plough.
128.	耳	R.	The ear.
129.	聿	Lŭh.	A pencil.
130.	肉 月	Juh.	Flesh.
131.	臣	Ch'eng.	A minister.
132.	自	Ts.	Self, from.
133.	至	Ch.	To, most.
134.	臼	Kiu.	A mortar.
135.	舌	Sheh.	The tongue.
136.	舛	Ch'üan.	Error.
137.	舟	Cheu.	A boat.
138.	艮	Keng.	Perverso.
139.	色	Seh.	Color.
140.	艸 艹	Ts'au.	Grass.
141.	虍	Hu.	A tiger.
142.	虫	Ch'ung.	Reptiles.
143.	血	Hüih.	Blood.
144.	行	Hing.	Walk, work.
145.	衣 衤	I.	Clothes.
146.	西 襾	Si.	West.

7 Strokes.

#	Char	Reading	Meaning
147.	見	Kien.	To see.
148.	角	Kioh.	Horn.
149.	言	Yien.	Words.
150.	谷	Kuh.	A valley.
151.	豆	Teu.	Beans.
152.	豕	Sh.	Swine.
153.	豸	hiai.	Reptiles, wild beasts.
154.	貝	Pe.	Pearls.
155.	赤	Ch'ih.	Scarlet.
156.	走	Tseu.	To walk.
157.	足	Tsuh.	The foot.
158.	身	Shin.	The body.
159.	車	Kŭ, ch'e.	A chariot.
160.	辛	Sing.	Acrid.
161.	辰	Ch'eng.	Hour.

ANALYTICAL READER.

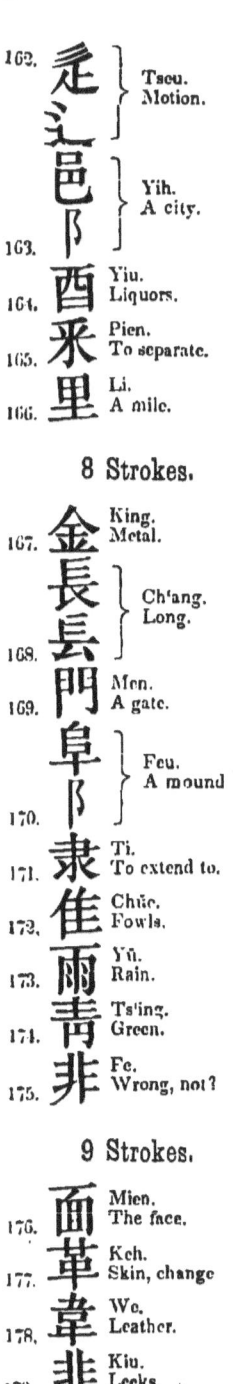

162. Tseu. Motion.
163. Yih. A city.
164. Yiu. Liquors.
165. Pien. To separate.
166. Li. A mile.

8 Strokes.

167. King. Metal.
168. Ch'ang. Long.
169. Men. A gate.
170. Feu. A mound.
171. Ti. To extend to.
172. Chŭe. Fowls.
173. Yŭ. Rain.
174. Ts'ing. Green.
175. Fe. Wrong, not?

9 Strokes.

176. Mien. The face.
177. Keh. Skin, change.
178. We. Leather.
179. Kiu. Leeks.

180. Ing. Sound.
181. Yih. Head, a leaf.
182. Fung. Wind, a custom.
183. Fe. To fly.
184. Shih. To eat.
185. Sheu. The head.
186. Hiang. Incense.

10 Strokes.

187. Ma. A horse.
188. Kuh. Bones.
189. Kau. High.
190. Piau. Long hair.
191. Teu. To quarrel.
192. Ch'ang. A fragrant liquor.
193. Keh, li. A tripod, urn.
194. Kwe. A ghost, a devil.

11 Strokes.

195. Yŭ. Fish.
196. Niau. A bird.
197. Lu. Brine.
198. Luh. A deer.
199. Meh. Wheat.
200. Ma. Hemp.

12 Strokes.

201. Hwang. Yellow.

202. Chu. Millet.
203. Heh. Black.
204. Ch'. Embroidery.

13 Strokes.

205. Ming. A Frog.
206. Ting. A Tripod.
207. Ku. A drum.
208. Ch'u. A Mouse.

14 Strokes.

209. Pih. The Nose.
210. Ts'i. Even, orderly.

15 Strokes.

211. Ch'. The teeth.
212. Lung. A Dragon.

16 Strokes.

213. Kwe. A tortoise.

17 Strokes.

214. Yuh. A Flute.

VOCABULARY.

1. 一

一 *i' (c), i i'* One.
上 *Shang',* Above, up, to go up.
且 *'Chie,* Moreover.
不 *Pu' (c) pu, pu',* Not.
七 *,Chi,* Seven.
世 *Shi',* The world, a generation
下 *Hia',* Below, to go down.
三 *,San,* Three.
丁 *'Ting,* A sting, a nail, an individual. to sustain.

2. 丨

中 *'Chung,* Middle, to hit the centre.

3. 丶

主 *'Chu,* Lord, to control
丸 *,Wan,* A ball, a pill.
丹 *,Tan,* Pale red, a sovreign remedy.

4. 丿

之 *,Chi,* Sign of possessive case, Pronoun of the 3rd person.
乃 *,Nai,* But, may-be, it is, i.e, viz.
乎 *,Hu,* A sign of doubt, admiration, inquiry; also of the vocative.

乘 *,Cheng,* A chariot, to ride, avail of, plot.
久 *'Chieu,* A long time.
乏 *Fu' (c) fu,* To want, lack,
么 *,Yau* 么麽 dwarfish,

5. 乙

乙 *'I i',* One, curved.
也 *,Ye,* Particle, sometimes interrogative, even, also.
亂 *Loan', lan,* Confusion, disorder.
九 *'Chieu,* Nine.
乳 *'Ju (c) nai,* Milk.

6. 亅

事 *Shi',* An act, affair, to serve.
予 *,U* Pronoun of 1st. person; to give.
了 *'Liau,* Finished, a sign of the past tense.

7. 二

二 *Ri',* Two.
云 *,Yün,* Speak say.
亞 *Ya',* Secondary. A diminutive prefix.
于 *,U,* In, in respect to.
五 *'Wu,* Five.

互 Hu⸴, Reciprocal.
況 K⸴wang⸴, Much more, a fortiori.
亟 Chi⸴ (c) ⸴chi, Haste, urgeney.

8. 亠

六 Lu⸴ (c) lieu, Six.
亦 I⸴, Also.
亡 ⸴Wang, Perish, lose, flee.
京 ⸴Ching, Great, the capital.
交 ⸴Chiau, Intercourse, alternate, reciprocal.
享 ʼHiang, Enjoy.

9. 人

人 ⸴Jen, Man.
來 ⸴Lai, Come.
作 Tso⸴, Make, start, arise.
使 ʼShi, Send, cause.
傳 ⸴Ch⸴wen, chwen⸴, Propagate, narrate.
伯 Pe⸴ (c) po, An uncle, a father's brother, a lord.
信 Hin⸴, Belief, faithfulness, a letter.
今 ⸴Chin, Now, modern.
以 ʼI, To take, accordingly.
但 Tan⸴, But, only.
僕 ʼP⸴u, Slave, servant.

何 ⸴Ho, Which? why? how?
儕 Ch⸴ai, Class, a plural suffix.
倫 ⸴Lun, A category social relations.
代 Tai⸴, A generation, instead of.
備 Pei⸴, Complete, prepared,
伏 Fu⸴, Prostrate, abject, to subject.
依 ⸴i, Depend on, according to.
仍 ⸴Jeng, jen, As before, still, yet.
儀 ⸴I, Ceremony, form, manner.
便 Pien⸴, Convenient, ready.
付 Fu⸴, Impart, intrust, pay.
令 Ling⸴, Command.
俯 ʼFu, To bow the head.
修 ⸴Hieu, Improve, cultivate: repair.
余 ⸴ü, Pron 1st. pers.
俊 Chün⸴, Superior, fine-looking.
俱 ⸴Chü, (c) chü, Together, all.
仇 Ch⸴ieu, Enmity.
仁 ⸴Jen, Humanity, charity, goodness.
僭 Chien⸴, False assumption, blasphemy.

VOCABULARY. 9

偽 Wei', False, deceitful.
例 Li', A custom
傾 ,Ch'ing, Overturn, a moment.
傷 ,Shang, Wound, bruise.
侍 Shï', Wait on, wait in presence.
他 T'o (c), T'a, (c) other, pron-3rd pers.
任 Jen', ,jen, Bear office or burden, ad libitum.
保 'Pau, Protect, secure.
伊 ,I, Pron, 3rd pers.
俾 Pi', To cause, so that.
偕 ,Hie, Together with.
供 ,Kung, kung', Serve, minister.
位 Wei', Seat, position person.
偶 'Ngeu, 'eu, Likeness, companion, pair.
像 Hiang', Like, simulacrum.
俗 Su' (c) ,su, Customary, common.
伐 Fa', Boast, cut, invade.
倘 T'ang, If, should.
侮 Wu, Insult.
佛 Fu', (c) ,fo, Budha.
係 Hi', To be, to concern.
傑 Chie', A hero.

值 Chi', (c) ,chi', Price, to meet, manage.
償 ,Chang, Pay, recompense.
休 ,Hieu, Stop, good fortune.
倍 Pei', Double, multiply.
億 I', Ten myriads, quiet, repose.
佑 Yeu', Divine protection.
俘 ,Fu, A captive.
俟 Sï', To wait for, until.
偏 ,P'ien, Uneven, partial.
側 Che' tso', Sloping, oblique.
侵 ,Chin, Usurp, oppress.
似 Sï', Like, resemble.
假 'Chia, False, to borrow, suppose.
倚 'I, Rely, lean on.
仗 Chang', Rely on, weapon, fight.
僅 'Chin, Exactly, only, scarcely.
舍 She', A cottage, to bestow, cast away.
住 Chu', Stop, dwell.
仰 'Yang, To look up.
伸 ,Shen, Extend, explain.
儘 Chin', Altogether, empty, as you please.

儔 ₂C‘heu, A class, a mate
僉 ₂C‘hien, All.
催 ₂Ts‘ui, Urge, expedite.
併 ₂Ping, (c) Ping⁴, Unite, 'combine energies.
佳 ₂Chia, Excellent.
僮 ₂T‘ung, Lad, urchin.
倜 ₂C‘heu, T‘iau, Free, noble.
儻 'T‘ang, If, should.
俠 Chia‘, Hia‘, generous, careless.
傲 Ngau‘, Proud, insolent.
伶 ₂Ling, A play actor, clever.
俐 Li‘, Smart.
佩 Pei‘, Side ornaments, to gird, wear at the side.
促 T‘su‘, Hasten, shorten.
借 Chie‘, Borrow.
佐 'Tso, Help.
儲 ₂C‘hu, Provide, store, to second.
件 Chien‘, A piece, or article.
候 Heu‘, Wait, inquire for, time.
侈 C‘hi‘, Wasteful.
介 Chie‘, Attendant, usher, shield, shellfish.
俄 ₂Ngo ₂o, Sudden, lofty.

伴 Pan‘, A comrade.
侶 'Lü, An associate.
傴 ₂Ngeu‘, ₂eu, stooping.
僂 ₂Leu, Crooked, bent.

10. 儿

先 ₂Hien, Before, first.
兄 ₂Hiung, Elder brother.
光 ₂Kwang, Light, bright.
免 'Mien, Avoid, forgive.
兆 Chau‘, An omen, a million.
兒 ₂Ri, (c) ₂Ri, A boy, child, a euphonic.
元 ₂Yuen, Primary, chief.
克 K‘o‘, Overbearing, to overcome.
允 'Yün, Promise, secure.
充 ₂C‘hung, Fill, pretend.

11. 入

入 Ju‘, To enter.
全 ₂C‘hiuen, Complete, perfect; all.
兩 'Liang, Two, both, a täel.
內 Nui‘, ‘Nei, Inside.

12. 八

八 (c) Pa‘ ₂pa, Eight.
兮 ₂Hi, A euphonic expletive.

其 ,C'hi, Pron, 3rd pers.
兵 ,Ping, A soldier, weapon.
公 ,Kung, Public, just, duke.
共 Kung‘, Together, in common.
具 Chü‘ Complete, instruments.
典 'Tien, A rule, to manage.
兼 ,Chien, To combine.
冀 Chi‘, Expect, desire.

13. 冂

再 Tsai‘, Again, the second time.

14. 冖

冠 ,Kwan‘, kwan, A cap, crown.
冥 ,Ming, Dark, obscure.

15. 冫

冷 ,Leng, Cold.
凌 ,Ling, Insult, spurn.
凋 ,Tiau, Wither.
冬 ,Tung, Winter, to freeze.
凄 ,C'hi, Chilly, grievous.

16. 几

凡 ,Fan, All, the world.
几 Chi‘, Bench, table.

17. 凵

出 C'hu‘, (c) ;c'hu‘, Out.

凸 ,Wei, ,tu (c) 'ku, Protuberance, a tenon.
凹 ,Yau (c) ,wa, A pit, valley.

18. 刀

前 ,C'hien, Before, formerly.
利 Li‘, Gain, advantage, sharp.
列 Lie‘, Numerous, several, clasified.
則 Tse‘, So, then.
刑 ,Hing, Punishment.
切 C'hie (c) ;c'hie, Divide, cut.
刃 Jen‘, A blade, a sharp edge.
別 Pie‘ (c) ,pie, Distinguish, other, don‘t
分 ,Fen, A part, duty.
割 Ko‘, (c) ,ko, To cut.
判 P'an‘, Divide, decide.
創 C'hwang‘, Originate, create, wound.
劍 Chien‘, A sabre.
刀 ,Tau, A knife, sword.
刻 K'o‘, (c) ,k'o, Carve, cut, griping, close, quarter of an hour, a moment.
制 Chi‘, Control, appoint, costume, mourning habit.
剛 ,Kang, Hard, steel.

刺 Ts'ï, Pierce, satirize.
劇 Chü‘, Excessive, increase, a farce.
劃 Hwa‘, Engrave, rend asunder.
刮 Kwa‘ (c) kwa, Scrape, include, embrace.
剖 P'eu, Divide.
刪 ‚Shan, To expurgate, amend.

19. 力

力 Li‘, Strength, force.
加 ‚Chia, Add, increase.
功 ‚Kung, Merit, attack.
勞 ‚Lau, Toil, to reward.
勒 Le‘, Extort, compel, curb, engrave.
勸 C'hiuen‘, Persuade, exhort.
助 Chu‘, Help.
動 Tung‘, Move.
勤 ‚C'hin, Industry, diligence.
勢 Shï‘, Force, power, posture of affairs.
勇 ’Yung, Valor, brave.
勵 Li‘, Stimulate.
勉 ’Mien, Encourage, earnest.

20. 勹

勿 Wu‘, Must not.

包 ‚Pau, Wrap up, comprehend.
匍 ‚P'u, Creep.
匐 ’Fu, Crouch.

21. 匕

北 Po‘ (c) pei‘, North.
化 Hwa‘, Transform reform, waste, flower.
比 ’P'i, ’pi, A spoon.

22. 匚

匱 Kwei‘, A Chest.
匪 ’Fei, Worthless, is not.

23. 匸

匿 Ni‘, Conceal, hide.
區 ‚C'hü, Place, space, room, empty.

24. 十

十 Shï‘ (c) ‚shï, Ten.
千 ‚C'hien, A thousand.
卒 Tsu‘, End, die, a soldier.
南 ‚Nan, South.
半 Pan‘, Half.
升 ‚Sheng, Ascend.
博 Po‘ (c) ‚po, Erudite.
井 ’Ching, Investigate, a well, market.

卑 ,Pei, Mean, lowly.
午 'Wu, Noon, the first hour.

25. 卜

卜 'Pu, To divine.
占 ,Chan, Chan', Observe auguries, usurp.

26. 冂

即 Chi', Then, even, i. e;
卷 Chiuen', A roll, part of a book.
印 Yin', Print, seal.
卵 'Loan, Eggs.

27. 厂

厥 C'hiue', Pron. of 3rd person.
原 ,Yuen, Original, of course.
厚 Heu', Thick, generous.
厭 Yen', Satiate, disgust.

28. 厶

矣 'I, An emphatic particle.
去 C'hü', Go, reject.
參 ,Ts'an, ,shen, A trine, together, worship.

29. 又

又 Yeu', Also, again.
取 'C'hü, To take.
及 Chi', (c) ,chi, Also, in addition.

受 Sheu', To receive.
友 'Yeu, A 'friend.
反 'Fan, Turn, contrary.
叛 P'an,' To rebel.

30. 口

口 'K'eu, Mouth.
和 ,Ho, Harmony, mix, together with.
命 Ming', Decree, fate, life.
善 Shan', Good.
告 Kaw, Inform, proclaim.
可 'K'o, Can, may.
名 ,Ming, Name.
問 Wen', Ask.
同 ,T'ung, Together, like.
各 Ko' (c) ,ko, Each, every.
司 ,Si, Control, manage.
嗣 Si', To inherit, succeed.
后 Heu', A sovereign, an empress.
君 ,Chiün. A king, a chief.
召 Chaw'. To summon.
哉 ,Tsai. A note of admiration.
向 Hiang'. Direction, towards.
呼 ,Hu, To call, to breathe.

否 'Feu, A negative alternative.
嘗 ‚C'hang, Taste, a sign of the past tense.
吾 ‚Wu Pron, 1st pers sing.
周 ‚Cheu, Circumference, complete.
哥 ‚Ko, Elder brother.
古 'Ku, Ancient.
史 'Shï, History.
喻 ü`, Comparison, to inform.
喪 ‚Sang, sang`, Decease, loss.
喜 'Hi, Pleasure.
咸 ‚Hien, All, entire.
吉 Chi`, (c) ‚chi, Good luck.
右 Yeu`, The right hand.
器 C'hi`, Vessel, instrument.
合 Ho`, (c) ‚ho, To join, agree.
單 ‚Tan, Single, a bill of particulars.
哭 ‚K'u, To weep, cry.
咎 Chieu`, Fault, sin.
嗜 Shï`, greedy, to.
哇 'Fa, Pha.
唎 Li`, Ri.
嚷 Sai`, See.
商 ‚Shang, Merchant, to consult.

嘉 ‚Chia, Excellent, auspicious.
哲 Che`, Wise, worthy.
吏 Li`, Officials.
叚 'Ku, Longevity.
嚴 ‚Yen, Severe, strict.
呪 Cheu`, To curse, incantation.
吹 ‚C'hui To blow.
吞 ‚T'un, To swallow.
噬 Shï`, To devour.
舌 She` (c) ‚she, The tongue.
售 Sheu`, To sell.
只 'Chi, Only.
品 'P'in, Class, grade, offerings.
呂 'Lü, A family name. a musical scale.
叩 K'eu`, Kotow, knock the head, knock at a door.
嘲 ‚C'hau, Ridicule.
吮 'Yün, Lick with the tongue.
咫 'Chi, A span.
唐 ‚T'ang, Name of a dynasty.
舍 ‚Han, To contain, hold in the mouth.
嘘 ‚Hü, Blow, puff.
咀 'Tsü, To chew.

嚼 Chio͘ (c) ͵chiau, To masticate.
唱 C͑hang͵, To sing.
吟 ͵Yin, To hum, cantillate.
喧 ͵Hiuen, Noise.
啟 ʼC͑hi, To open, begin.

31. 口

四 Sz͘, Four.
因 ͵Yin, Because, from.
國 Kwe͘ (c) ͵kwe, Kingdom, nation.
回 ͵Hwei, Turn, return.
圖 ͵T͑u, A map, to plot.
固 Ku͘, Firm, of course.
園 ͵Yuen, A garden.
困 K͑wen͘, Press, oppress.
圍 ͵Wei, Invest, besiege, around.
囚 ͵C͑hieu, A prisoner.
囿 Yeu͘, A park, garden.

32. 土

土 ʼT͑u, Ground, earth, opium.
地 Tiʹ, The earth, ground, a place.
基 ͵Chi, Foundation, estate.
在 Tsai͘, In, on, at.
城 ͵C͑heng, A city, a wall.

垂 ͵C͑hui, To condescend, let down.
境 Ching͘, Peace, region.
垣 ͵Yuen, A wall.
執 Chiʹ, To hold, control, take.
報 Pau͘, To report, recompense.
埃 ͵Yai, The soil, ground.
堂 ͵T͑ang, A hall.
墓 Mu͘, A tomb, grave.
壤 ʼJang, Ground, soil.
坐 Tso͘ʹ To sit.
壇 ͵T͑an, An altar.
墮 To͘, To fall.
塗 ͵T͑u, To daub, mortar.
塵 ͵C͑hen, Dust, earth.
場 ͵C͑hang, Open ground.
坦 ʼT͑an, Level ground.
坷 ͵K͑o, Uneven ground.
圮 ʼC͑hi, Crumbling, shattered.
壞 Hwaiʹ, Spoiled, ruined.
堅 ͵Chien, Firm, solid.
塞 Se͘, saiʹ, To stop up.
增 ͵Tseng, To add, increase.
塔 ʼT͑a, A tower.
均 ͵Chiün, All, equal.

堪 ,K'an, May, can, endure.
塹 Chan', A pit, a ravine.
堦 ,Chie, Stairway.
塾 Shu' (c) ,shu, A school.
塒 ,Shi, A coop for fowls.

33. 士

士 Shi', A scholar.
壯 Chwang', A bed.
壽 Sheu', Age, longevity.

34. 夂

夏 Hia', Summer, name of a dynasty, of China.

36. 夕

多 ,To, Much, many.
夕 Hi' (c) ,hi, Evening.
夢 Mong', A dream.
夜 Ye', Night.
外 Wai', Outside.
夙 Su' Early, north.

37. 大

大 Ta' tai', Great.
天 ,T'ien, Heaven.
夫 ,Fu, A man, husband, fu-ts a teacher, fu-jin, a lady. fu, a euphonic particle.
太 T'ai' Grand, vast.

奠 Tien', Fix, establish, to make a libation.
奈 Nai', ngai', How!
奮 Fen', Earnest, energetic.
奬 'Chiang, To praise, exhort.
奧 Ngau', Mysterious.
夾 Chiu' (c) ,chia, To approach from both sides.
奕 I', Vast, to gamble.

39. 女

奉 Feng', Obey, receive orders.
失 Shi' (c) ,shi, To lose.
奪 To' (c) ,to, Snatch, seize.
奇 ,C'hi, Rare, wonderful.
奚 ,Hi, How? why? a page, a maid.
奔 ,Pen, To run.
奏 Tseu', A report or memorial to the sovereign, to strike up music.
女 'Nü, A woman, a daughter.
如 ,Ju, As, like, if.
妻 ,Chi, A wife,
始 'Shi, Beginning.
嫩 Nun', Tender, fresh.
好 'Hau, Good.
妄 Wang', False, deceitful.

VOCABULARY. 17

婦 Fuʻ, Woman, wife.
娶 ʻChü, To marry.
姓 Hingʻ, The family name, the family.
嬰 ˏYing, An infant.
姊 ʼTsi, ʼchie, ʼchi, Elder sister.
妹 Meiʻ, Younger sister.
奴 ˏNu, A slave.
婢 Piʻ, A maid servant.
嫁 Chiaʻ, To give in marriage.
威 ˏWei, Dignity, majesty, prowess.
姑 ˏKu, A maiden, an aunt, a wife's mother-in-law.
妙 Miauʻ, Admirable,
妥 ʼTʻo, Complete, satisfactory.
娛 ˏü, Delight.
妍 ˏYen, Elegant, refined, delicate.
媚 Meiʻ, Pretty, charming.

39. 子

子 ʼTs Son, child, doctor.
字 Tsiʻ, Letters, the marriage name, to love, nourish.
孰 Shu, Who? which?
存 ˏTsun, To retain, preserve, continue.

孫 ˏSun, A grandson, gentle, yielding.
孩 ˏHai A child.
孝 Hiauʻ, Filial piety.
季 Chiʻ, A season, the last of three.
孕 Yünʻ, Pregnant.
孳 ˏTsi, To multiply, to swarm.

40. 宀

宜 ˏI, Proper, fitting, to set in order.
家 ˏChia, A family.
安 ˏNgan, Rest, quiet.
守 ʼSheu, To hold, maintain,
實 Shiʻ (c) ˏshi, Solid, real.
容 ˏYung, The face, to tolerate.
室 Shiʻ, A chamber, a house.
宮 ˏKung, A palace.
宰 ʼTsai, A ruler, to slay.
定 Tingʻ, Certain, to fix, determine.
害 Haiʻ, To harm, injure.
宣 ˏHiuen, To proclaim, publish.
寢 ˏCʻhin, To go to bed, to sleep.
審 ʼShen, To examine, judge.

宇 ,ü, A roof, house, the canopy of heaven.
富 Fu‛, Rich.
宗 ,Tsung, Ancestor, chief, oracle.
察 Ch‛a‛, Search, examine, investigate.
寶 'Pau, Precious.
冤 ,Yuen, Injury, spleen, blame.
官 ,Kwan, Officer, mandarin, to govern.
寅 ,Yien, To reverence; the 3rd. of the 12 hours.
客 K‛o‛, A guest, stranger, merchant, customer.
寧 ,Ning, Tranquil, rather.
寬 ,K‛wan, Large, generous, indulgent.
宏 ,Hung, Great, vast.
密 Mi‛, Close, secret, intimate.
寵 'Ch‛ung, Favor, affection.
寡 'Kwa, Destitute, few, a widow.
宿 Su‛ ,hü, A constellation, to pass a night, lodge.
宥 Yeu‛, Indulge, pardon.
寒 ,Han, Cold, frigid.
寰 ,Hwan, The globe, a circuit.
寄 Chi‛, To lodge, convey, a remainder.

41. 寸

寸 Tsun‛, An inch.
將 ,Chiang, Take command, intend, will be or do.
導 Tau‛, To lead.
尊 ,Tsun, To respect, reverence.
對 Tui‛, Opposite, a pair, to compare.
專 ,Chwen, Special, sale.
尋 ,Hiün, To seek, afterwards.
封 ,Feng, To seal, appoint.
射 She‛, To shoot.

42. 小

小 'Hiau, Small.
少 'Shau, Few, young.
尚 Shang‛, Ch‛ang, Above, to exalt, yet.

43. 尢

就 Ch‛ieu,‛ Then, thereon, come to.
尤 ,Yeu, Blame, fault, more.

44. 尸

尼 ,Ni Near, familiar.
居 ,Chü, To dwell, locate.

屋 Wu⁽ (c) ₂wu, A house.
屬 ʼShu, To belong to, to enjoin.
履 ʼLü, Sandals, to walk, an income.
尸 ₂Shi, A corpse, an effigy.
屍 ₂Shi, A dead body.
尺 ʼCh'i, A foot, a rule.
屆 Chie⁽, To reach, arrive at.
屢 ʼLü, Often, repeatedly.
層 ₂Ts'eng, A story, or stratum.

46. 山

山 ₂Shan, Hill, mountain.
崇 ₂Ch'ung, Lofty, to reverence.
巖 ₂Yien, A cliff, precipice.
島 ʼTau, An island.
岡 ₂Kang, A steep high hill.
岸 Ngan⁽, A shore, bank.
崩 ₂Peng, To fall, death of a prince.
崙 ₂Lun, A peak, summit.
嵐 ₂Lan, The atmosphere.
崎 ₂Ch'i, Rough, uneven.
嶇 ₂Ch'ü, Rugged.
崖 ₂Yai, A steep bank, a cliff.
峽 Chia⁽, A mountain pass, a strait.

岱 Tai⁽, The Taishan mts.
嶽 Yo⁽, A mountain.
嶔 ₂Ch'in, Lofty, sublime.
嶷 Ngai⁽, ai⁽, A dizzy height.
嶂 Chang⁽, A chain of hills.
峥 ₂Cheng, Eminent.
嶸 ₂Yung, Conspicuous.
峰 ₂Feng, A peak.

47. 川

州 ₂Cheu, An island, continent, district.
川 ₂Ch'wen, A stream.
巢 ₂Ch'au, A nest, a lair.

48. 工

工 ₂Kung, Work, mechanism.
左 ʼTso, The left hand, wrong, to aid.
巨 Ch'ü⁽, Huge, chief.
差 ₂Ch'a, ₂ch'ai, Difference, error.
巧 ʼCh'iau, Skilful, cunning.

49. 己

己 ʼI, Already, to stop, a euphonic final.
巴 ₂Pa, A grip, handful, blow, name of a place, sign of the optative.

己 'Chi, Self, reflex pron.

50. 巾

巾 ,Chin, A turban, cap, kerchief.

帝 Ti', A ruler, supreme majesty.

希 ,Hi, To expect, rare.

慕 Mu', Tent, tabernacle.

師 ,Shi, A master, army, multitude.

布 Pu', Cotton cloth, to spread abroad.

常 ,C'hang, Constant, always, common.

市 Shi', A market.

席 Hi', (c) ,hi, Matting, feast, meal.

帶 Tai', A belt, draw, convey.

帕 P'a', A Hood, a stomacher.

帛 Pe', Silk stuff, wealth, money.

51. 干

年 ,Nien, A year.

干 ,Kan, A shield, to offend, serious consequences.

并 Ping', United, also, even.

平 ,P'ing, Level, just.

52. 幺

幾 ,Chi, 'chi, How, almost.

幼 Yeu', Tender, youth, young.

幽 Yeu', Gloomy, dismal.

幻 Hwan', Transform, sleight of hand.

53. 广

庇 'P'i, To protect.

底 'Ti, Bottom.

廣 ,Hwang, Broad.

庶 Shu', All, almost.

廢 Fei', To set aside, waste.

度 Tu', A degree, to measure, estimate.

座 Tso', A seat, throne.

府 'Fu, A mansion.

庸 ,Yung, Constant, common, to employ.

庫 K'u', Treasury.

康 ,K'ang, Tranquil.

廊 ,Lang, Portico, verandah.

序 Hu', Preface, order, a college.

庠 ,Hiang, Academy, asylum.

廚 ,C'hu, A kitchen.

廁 Si‛, A privy, to cleanse.
厫 Chieu‛, Stable.
庥 ‚Hieu, To protect.
庖 ‚P‛au, Kitchen, butcher's stall.
庭 ‚T‛ing, A hall.

54. 廴

建 Chien‛, To build, lay a foundation.
延 ‚Yen, To prolong, to invite.
廻 ‚Hwei, To turn back.

55. 弋

弋 I‛, An arrow.
式 Shi‛, A model, a prop to lean on.

57. 弓

強 ‚C‛hiang, ’c‛hiang, Strong, violent.
張 ‚Chang, Extend, stretch, bend.
弗 Fu‛, Not.
弟 Ti‛, Younger brother, disciple.
引 ’Yin, To lead, introduction.
弓 ‚Kung, A bow.
弱 Jo‛, Weak, feeble.
彈 ‚Tan, Beat a harp, a ball.

彌 ‚Mi, More and more.

59. 彡

形 ‚Hing, Form, body.
彰 ‚Chang, Display, luminous, illustrate.
彩 ’Ts‛ai, Brilliant, ornate.
影 ’Ying, Shaddow.

60. 彳

復 Fu‛, Return, again.
往 ’Wang, To go.
得 Te‛ (c) ‚tei, Obtain, get, can.
彼 ’Pi, That, adj. pron.
從 ‚Ts‛ung, Follow, from.
徒 ‚T‛u, Disciple, in vain, only.
後 Heu‛, After, posterity.
役 I‛, To serve, a low official, police runner.
微 ‚Wei, Minute, subtile.
待 Tai‛, Treat, wait.
循 ‚Hiün, Observe, according to.
德 Te‛ (c) ‚te, Virtue.
征 ‚Cheng, Advance, invade, conquer.
徵 ‚Cheng, To test, examine, act.
徑 Ching‛, A path.

徜 ₂T'ang, Loll, stroll, lounge.
徉 ₂Yang, Roving, straying.
徐 ₂Hü, Gradual, at leisure.

61. 心

心 ₂Hin, Heart.
惟 ₂Wei, Only, but, think.
惡 Ngo', wu', Evil, hate.
愛 Ngai', ai', Love.
意 I', Thought, intention.
必 Pi' (c) ₂pi, Certainly, must.
性 Hing', Nature.
感 'Kan, Feel, excite feeling.
忽 Hu' (c) ₂hu, Sudden.
忍 ²Jen, Cruel, patient.
恐 ₂K'ung, Apprehension, lest.
悔 ²Hwei, Regret, repent.
悅 Yue', Please, be pleased.
悉 Hi' (c) ₂hi, All, to investigate.
惑 Hwo', hu', Tempt, doubt, waver.
愚 ₂U, Dull, stupid.
患 Hwan', Affliction.
憂 ₂Yeu, Sorrow, grief.
懼 Ch'ü', Dread.
怒 Nu', Anger.

忘 ₂Wang, Forget.
恃 Shï', To rely on.
恩 ₂En, ngen, Grace.
恤 Hü', Favor, mercy, pity.
志 Chï', Inclination, will, history, to record.
念 Nien', Thought, to read.
情 ₂Ching, Passions, affairs, natural feelings.
息 Hi', Rest, cease.
愈 U', Better, to heal.
恒 ₂Heng, Persevering, permanent.
懷 ₂Hwai, Bosom, to feel, cherish.
恭 ₂Kung, Respect.
暴 Pau', Violence, oppression.
愆 ₂C'hien, Guilt.
應 ₂Ying, ying', Answer, ought.
思 ₂Si, To think.
憫 ²Min, Compassion.
慧 Hwei', Smartness, wisdom.
慈 ₂T'si, Mercy, tenderness.
憑 ₂P'ing, Proof, to rest on,
憾 Han', Hate, dislike.
急 Chï', (c) ₂chi, Haste, urgency.

欲 Ü‘, Passion, desire, appetite.
慎 Shen‘, Cautious, precise.
想 ’Hiang, To think, desire.
悟 Wu‘, Conscious, awake.
慮 Lü‘, To care for.
懽 ‚Hwan, Pleasure.
惠 Hwei‘, Comfort, kindness.
憐 ‚Lien, Pity, love.
惜 Hi‘ (c) ‚hi, Regret, spare, love.
慰 Wei‘, Soothe, support.
忠 ‚Chung, Loyal, faithful.
恪 C‘hio‘, Dignified.
恨 Hen‘, Hate, abhor.
憶 I‘, Think of, remember, conjecture.
慢 Man‘, Slow, disrespect.
慄 Li‘, Tremble, dread.
怨 Yuen‘, Blame, complaint, hate.
懸 ‚Hiuen, Suspend.
忿 Fen‘, Anger, rage.
忙 ‚Mang, Hurried, busy.
慕 Mu‘, Desire, admire.
懺 ‚Chien, ‚chan, Repent, a penitential prayer.

悮 Ü‘, Mistake, error.
怱 ‚Tsung, Haste.
忻 ‚Hin, Delight.
慶 C‘hing‘, Felicity.
恥 ’C‘hi, Shame,
戀 Lien‘, To dote.
快 K‘wai‘, Quick, joyous.
忖 ’Ts‘un, Think, suspect.
悚 ’Sung, Awe.
惶 ‚Hwang, Dread, apprehension,
慌 ‚Hwang, Hurry, confused.
慝 T‘e‘, Fault, evil, badness.
惕 T‘i‘, Reverence.
慙 ‚Ts‘an, Shame.
懟 Tui‘, Vexation, hate.
悛 ‚C‘hiuen, Reform.

62. 戈

或 Hwo‘, Or, either, suppose, some one.
我 ’Ngo, (c) ’wo, I, pron. 1st pers.
成 ‚C‘heng, Complete.
戮 Lu‘, Cut to pieces.
戰 Chan‘, Fight, battle.
戈 ‚Ko, A pike, a weapon.

戒 *Chie',* To Caution, forbid, renounce.
戚 *C'hi',* A relative, sorrow.
戴 *Tai',* Wear, or bear on the head.
戛 *Chia',* A lance, jolting, stammering, usual.

63. 戶

戶 *Hu',* A door, family, owner.
戾 *Lei',*
房 *,Fang,* House, room.

64. 手

手 *'Sheu,* Hand.
摩 *,Mo,* (c) *,mo,*
拿 *,Na,* Take, seize.
撒 *Sa'* (c) *,sa,* (c) *'sa,* scatter.
拉 *,La,* Draw.
拯 *'Cheng,* Save, succor.
拜 *Pai',* Worship, bow down.
按 *An',* According to.
挪 *,No,* Rub, move, elude.
投 *,T'eu,* Plunge, cast.
舉 *'Chü,* Elevate, all.
指 *'Chi,* Point, finger.
押 *Ya'*(c)*,ya,*Pawn, seal, compel.

攜 *,Hi, ,hie,* Convey, carry.
擊 *Chi',* Strike.
掃 *,Sau,* Sweep.
據 *Chü',* Hold, proof.
揚 *,Yang,* Spread, display.
接 *Chie'* (c) *,chie,* Receive, accept, connect with.
捫 *,Men,* Handle, feel with the hand.
援 *,Yuen,* Rescue, succor.
招 *,Chau,* To beckon, call together.
播 *Po',* Scatter, winnow.
提 *,T,i,* Handle, take up.
抵 *,Ti,* Oppose, balance.
拒 *Chü',* Resist.
才 *,Ts'ai,* Talent, ability.
授 *Sheu',* Entrust, impart.
扶 *,Fu,* Sustain.
持 *,C'hi,* Hold, control.
擇 *Cho',* (c) *,chai,* Choose, select.
推 *,T'ui,* Push.
抑 *I'.* Or, either, rule, repress.
抹 *'Mo.* Wipe, blot, paint.
操 *,Ts'au, ts'au,* Hold fast, manage.

掌 ,Chang The palm, hold, control.

攘 ,Jang, steal.

承 ,C'heng, Receive, accept, thanks.

捐 ,Chiuen, Contribute, sacrifice.

抱 Pau', Nurse, embrace, hug.

搖 ,Yau, Shake, rock, skull a boat.

撻 'Ta, Whip, scourge.

打 'Ta, Strike, beat.

擬 ,Ni, Decide, condemn.

折 Cho' (c) ,cho, Break open, take apart.

捕 'P'u, Capture, seize.

振 Chen', Arouse, stir up.

擲 Chi' (c) ,chi, Cast, throw.

搴 ,C'hien, Pluck, snatch.

探 T'an', ,t'an, Test, try, sound, inquire.

抄 ,C'hau, Transcribe, copy, take, confiscate.

拓 To', Open, inaugurate.

攀 ,P'an, Cling, hold to.

排 ,P'ai, Arrange, spread out.

披 ,P'i, Cover, cloak.

掩 'Yen, Veil, conceal.

挽 'Wan, Draw back.

揮 ,Hwei, Wield, manage.

拊 'Fu, Beat, play on a harp.

拍 ,P'ai, (c) p'o', Pat, tap.

擎 Chi', Choose, hinder, compel.

採 'Ts'ai, Pick up, cull.

拔 Pa', c ,pa, Pluck up, assist.

拾 Shi', (c) ,shi Gather, pick up.

撥 C'ho', Break, snap.

擷 Chie', Strip, break.

掬 Chü', Handful, to take with both hands.

撈 ,Lau, (c) ,lau, Grasp, seize.

抛 ,P'au, Cast, throw away.

搏 ,T'oan, Knead, compress.

挈 Sie, Carry in the hand.

65. 支

支 ,Chi, Diverge, give, pay, prop, succor.

66. 支

敵 Ti', (c) ,ti, Rival, enemy.

致 Chi', To cause, so that, investigate

故 Ku', A cause, reason, therefore.

教 Chiau⁵, ₅chiau, Teach, doctrine, religion.
救 Chieu⁵, Save.
數 Shu⁵, Number, destiny.
改 'Kai, Change, reform.
敢 'Kan, Dare.
攻 ₅Kung, Merit, attack.
敬 Ching⁵, Respect, reverence.
敗 Pai⁵, Defeat, waste.
散 San⁵, ₅san,· Scatter.
政 Cheng⁵, Government, politics.
收 ₅Sheu, Receive, collect.
放 Fang⁵, Release, let loose.
攷 'K'au, Examine, search.
敷 ₍Fu, (c) ₍fu, Spread, diffuse.

67. 文
文 ₍Wen, Literature, Figures.
斐 'Fei, Elegant.

68. 斗
斗 'Teu, A peck measure, the Great Bear.
料 Liau⁵, Materiel, to conjecture.

69. 斤
所 'So, Which, what, where.

斯 ₅Sī, This.
斷 Toan⁵, Cut, break, by all means.
斥 C̱hi⁵, Rebuke.
新 ₍Sin, New, renew,
斤 ₍Chin, A catty, an axe.

70. 方
方 ₍Fang, Square, place, method, thereon,
族 Tsu⁵ ₍tsu, Family clan.
於 ₍U, In, on, pertaining to.
旁 ₍P'ang, Side.
施 ₍Shī, Give.
旅 'Lū, Stranger, company, batallion.
旋 ₍Hiuen, Revolve, in turn.

71. 无
既 Chī⁵, Since, already.
无 ₍Wu, Without, privative.

72. 日
日 Jī⁵, Sun, a day.
昔 Hī⁵ (c) ₍hi, Formerly, anciently.
明 ₍Ming, Bright, understand.
是 Shī⁵, To-morrow, to be, right.
時 ₍Shi, Time, hour.

昭 ,Chau, Shine, display.
智 Chï, Wisdom.
旨 'Chi, Will, taste.
暗 An', Dark.
易 I, Change, easy.
昧 Mei', Obscure, blinded.
晝 Cheu', Noon, daytime.
晚 'Wan, Evening, night.
早 'Tsau, Early.
曠 K'wang', Barren; desert.
昆 ,K'wun, Elder brother, a worm.

普 'P'u, Far and wide.
晨 ,Chen, Morning, early.
星 ,Hing, A star.
昌 ,C'hang, Prosperous.
暫 Chan', Brief, temporary.
暮 Mu', Evening, twilight.
替 T'i, Instead, fail.
暨 Chï, Also, more.
暢 C'hang', Flourishing, comfortable.
晴 ,C'hing, Clear.
陽 ,Yang, Bright, fair.
旱 Han', Dry weather.

春 ,C'hun, Spring.
晷 'Kwei, Sun dial.
晏 Yen'; Evening.
曉 'Hiau, Morning.
晰 Hi', Bright, discriminate.
映 Ying', Shine on, reflect image.
暖 'Noan, Warm; mild.
景 'Ching, Admirable, picturesque.
旦 Tan', Morning.
旬 ,Hiün, Ten days, a good term for a week.

73. 日

曰 Yue', Speak, said, called.
會 Hwei', Meet, can.
書 ,Shu, Write, book.
曹 ,Tsau, Class, sign of plural.
會 ,Tseng ,tseng, Sign of past tense, a family name.
最 Tsui', Most.
更 ,Keng keng', Change, more.
曲 C'hü' (c) ,C'hü C'hü, Crooked, injury.
曷 Ho', Why not?
曳 Ye', hie', Drag.

74. 月

有 'Yeu, Indulge, forgive.
月 Yuĕ, Moon, month.
望 Wang', Look towards, hope.
朝 ‚Chau, ‚chau, Morning, towards, palace, do homage.
勝 Sheng', Conquer, bear, surpass.
期 ‚C'hi, ‚chi, Period, expect.
服 Fu', (c) ‚fu, Submit, hug.
朋 ‚P'eng, Friend.
朔 So', North, first of a month.

75. 木

未 Wei', Not yet.
相 ‚Hiang hiang', Mutual, together.
木 Mu', Wood, timber.
本 'Pen, Root, origin.
東 ‚Tung, East.
樹 Shu', Tree, to plant.
果 'Kwo, Fruit, really.
榮 ‚Yung, Glory.
樂 Lo', yo', Yo', Joy, music.
集 Chi' (c) ‚chi, Collect.
極 Chi' (c) ‚chi, Extreme, limit.
棄 C'hi', Reject, leave, cast away.

業 Ye', Business, property, finally.
權 ‚Ch'iuen, Authority, a steelyard weight, an exception.
末 Mo' (c) mie', Tree top, end, tip end, no more, worthless.
架 Chia', Frame.
條 T'iau, A rod, a classifier of long things, an article, a law.
束 Shu', Bind.
概 Kai', A stable.
機 ‚Chi", Engine, opportunity.
植 ‚Chi, Plant, fix.
根 ‚Ken, Root.
横 ‚Heng, heng', Perverse, crosswise.
棘 (c) ‚Chi, Thorns, brambles.
枝 ‚Chi", A branch.
杯 ‚Pei, A cup.
橄 'Kan, Chinese olive, it belongs to the terebinthaceae.
欖 'Lan, A kind of olive, the canarium.
板 'Pan, Plank, board.
柱 Chu', Pillar, prop.
樣 Yang' Sample, pattern.
樓 ‚Leu, Loft, story.
枯 ‚K'u, Withered.

核 Ho‛, (c) ‚ho, Seed, kernel, compare, search.
格 Ko‛, (c) ‚ko, Reform, come.
杖 Chang‛, staff, cudgel.
某 ’Meu, Any, a certain one.
模 ‚Mu, Pattern, sample.
楷 ’C‛hiai, Model.
林 ‚Lin, Forest, grove.
榭 Hie‛, Terrace, arbor.
檻 ’K‛an, Railing, cage.
楣 ‚Mei, Door lintel.
構 Keu‛, Join, truss of a house.
材 ‚Ts‛ai, Materials.
榻 T‛a‛, A couch.
楮 ’C‛hu, Paper mulberry.
楊 ‚Yang, } Willow.
柳 ’Lieu. }
梧 ‚Wu, } The eleococcus, olcifera, t‛ung-yiu,
桐 ‚T‛ung, } wood oil.
桃 ‚T‛au, Peach.
李 ’Li, Plum, hing-li, baggage.
松 ‚Sung, Pine, fir.
栢 Po‛ (c) ’pai, Cedar, cypress.
柵 Cha‛, (c)‚cha, Stockade, railing.

76. 欠

欠 Chien‛, Lack, owe, debt.
欲 Ü‛, Wish, desire, will.
次 Ts‛‛i, Order, next in order.
歟 Ü, A final particle.
歡 ‚Hwan, Joy, to like.
欣 ‚Hin, Delight.
欺 ‚C‛hi, Deceive, insult.
歌 ‚Ko, A song.
謳 ‚Ngeu, Sing, chant, recite.

77. 止

此 ’Ts‛‛i, This.
歸 ‚Kwoi, Return, render, yield belong.
止 ’Chi, Stop, cease, only.
歷 Li‛, Pass over, away, successive, experience.
正 Cheng‛, (c) ‚cheng, Upright, virtuous.
武 ’Wu, Military, used for *pu*, a step.
歲 Sui‛, A year, season.
步 Pu‛, Step.
歧 ‚C‛hi, Diverge, *c‛hi lu* a bye way.

78. 歹

歹 ˈTai, Evil, bad.
死 ˈSǐ, Death.
殊 ˌShu, Different, really.
殘 ˌTsʻan, Cruel, barbarous.
殲 ˌChien, Kill destroy, perish.
殆 Taiʼ, Insecure, imminent, almost.
殤 Shang, Untimely death.
殂 ˈTsu, Dissolution, death.

79. 殳

殳 ˌShu, A spear.
殺 Shaʻ, (c) ˌsha, To kill.
殿 Tienʻ, Temple.
毀 ˈHwei, Destroy.
殷 ˌYin, Zealous, great.
般 ˌPan, A kind, the same.
殼 Cʻhioʻ, Shell, husk.

80. 毋

毋 ˌWu, ˌwu, Do not, a denial.
母 ˈMu, Mother.
每 ˈMei, Each, every.
毒 Tuʼ, (c) ˌtu Poison.
毓 Ǔʼ, Cherish, nurture, train.

81. 比

比 ˈPi, To compare.

82. 毛

毛 ˌMau, Hair, wool.
毫 ˌHau hair, down, a mote.

83. 氏

民 ˌMin, People, a plebeian.
氏 Shǐʼ, Family, suffix to a woman's name.

84. 气

氣 Cʻhiʼ, Breath, any gaseous body, matter, anger.

85. 水

水 ˈShui, Water.
求 ˌChieu, Seek, desire, pray.
法 Faʼ faʻ ˌfa, Law, mode, method.
溫 ˌWen, Tepid, warm, mild, gentle.
汝 ˈju, Thou.
沒 Moʻ, meiʻ, Sink, die, not, no, name.
深 ˌShen, Deep.
洗 ˈHi, To wash.
河 ˌHo, River, canal.
治 ˌCʻhi chǐʼ, Govern, manage.

沙 ,Shu, Sand.
洲 ,Cheu, Island, continent.
派 P'ai‘, Divide, appoint.
海 'Hai, The sea.
污 ,Wu, Filthy.
滅 Mie‘, Quench destroy.
潔 ₂Chie, Cleanse, purity.
波 ₂Po, A wave.
活 Hwo‘ (c) ₂hwo, Alive, mobile, lively.
酒 'Chieu, Wine.
油 ₂Yeu, Oil.
流 ₂Lieu, Flow, glide.
永 'Yung, Long, for ever.
濟 Chi‘, Cross a ferry, to give charity.
淫 ₂Yin, Adulterous, profligate, excess.
泣 Ch'i‘, To weep.
清 ₂Ch'ing, Pure, clear.
洪 ₂Hung, Great, vast.
沾 ,Chan, Moisten, tinge, infect.
濯 Cho‘, Wash, wash the feet.
沐 Mu‘, Bathe, bathe the head, receive favor.
漸 Chien‘, Gradual.

泥 ₂Ni, Mud.
澤 Che‘, A pool, favor.
灌 Kwun‘, Pour, irrigate.
泉 C'hiuen, Fountain, money.
江 ,Chiang, River.
洋 ₂Yang, Ocean.
滿 'Man, Full.
源 ₂Yuen, Source, fountain.
湖 ₂Hu, Lake,
漢 Han‘, Name of a river, of a dynasty, of the Chinese.
沉 ₂C'hen, To drown, sink, perish.
淪 ₂Lun, Eddy, gulf, sink, perish.
渴 'K'o, Thirst.
濱 ,Pin, Bank, brink,.
溯 So‘, Trace up, go against the current.
漏 Leu‘, Leak, omit.
渡 Tu‘, Ferry, to cross over.
消 ,Hiau, Melt, waste away.
潦 'Lau, Flood, excess of rain.
浮 ₂Feu, Float, swim, superficial.
渭 Wei‘, Name of a turbid river.
津 ,Chin, A ford, ferry.

涉 She‘, To wade, concern.
潮 C‘hau, Tide, damp.
潢 ‚Hwang, A lake, pool; chùang hwang, embellishment.
洛 Lo‘. }
泗 Sï‘. } Names of rivers.
淋 ‚Lin, Drip, trickle.
湍 ‚T‘wan, A torrent.
激 Chï‘, Excite, impede.
濫 Lan‘, A flood, excess, intrusive.
測 Che‘, Fathom, estimate, measure.
泰 T‘ai‘, Vast, quiet, opulent.
渚 ›Chu, An islet, sandbank.
淬 Tsui‘, To dip, dye.
泅 ‚Hieu, To swim.
濕 ‚Shi, (c) shï‘, Wet, damp, moist.
涕 T‘ï‘, To weep.
涙 Lei‘, Tears.
浩 Hau‘, Vast.
淵 ‚Yuen, Abyss.
滋 ‚Chï, To multiply.

86. 火

火 ’Hwo, Fire.
無 ‚Wu, Not.
焉 ‚Yen, Euphonic.
爲 ‚Wei, Be, become, make, do.
然 ‚Jan, So, yet.
營 ‚Ying, Plan, plot, camp, legion.
焚 ‚Fen, Consume.
烈 Lie‘, Fierce, brave.
烏 ‚Wu, A crow, black, what? where?
災 ‚Tsai, Calamity.
燔 ‚Fan, Burn.
烟 ‚Yen, Smoke, tobacco.
燬 ’Hwei, Destroy,
燃 ‚Jan, Kindle,
燈 ‚Teng, A Lamp.
照 Chau‘, Shine, enlighten.
熱 Jo‘, Heat.
勳 ‚Hiün, Merit.
煩 ‚Fan, Vex, perplex, trouble.
燮 Hie‘, Temper, mingle, blend.
燕 Yen‘, ‚yen.
熾 Chï‘, Kindle.
焰 Yen‘, Flame.
爍 Sho‘, Flash, explode.
燦 ’Ts‘an, Brilliant.

爛 Lan‘, Bright, torn, rotten.
煇 ‚Hwei, Splendor.
煌 ‚Hwang, Lustre.
烹 ‚P‘eng, Bake, roast.
熙 ‚Hi, Bright, glorious.
煮 ’Chu, Boil, cook.

87. 爪
爭 ‚Cheng, Contend, strive.
爰 ‚Yuen, Therefore, at, in, next.
爵 Chio‘, (o) ‚chio, Rank, title, office.

88. 父
父 Fu‘, Father.
爺 ‚Ye, Father, combined in various titles.

89. 爻
爾 ’Rĭ, Thou, a particle.

90. 爿
牀 ‚Chwang, Bed, bedstead.

91. 片
片 P‘ien‘, A strip, slip, leaf.
牖 Yeu‘, Door, window, to instruct.

92. 牙
牙 ‚Ya Teeth.

93. 牛
物 Wu‘, Thing, animal.
牛 ‚Nieu, Cow, ox.
牡 ’Mu, Male.
特 T‘e‘, Special, intentional, an ox.
犢 Tu‘, (c) ‚tu, A calf.
牧 Mu‘, Shepherd, herdsman.
牽 ‚C‘hien, Lead, draw.
牲 ‚Sheng, Cattle, beasts for sacrifice.
牢 ‚Lau, Firm, prison, a victim for sacrifice.

94. 犬
猶 ‚Yeu, Yet, like.
獄 Ŭ‘, Prison, law suit.
獸 Sheu‘, Wild beast.
獻 Hien‘, Present, offer.
犯 Fan‘, Violate, offend.
獲 Hwo‘, hu‘, Take, obtain.
獨 Tu‘, (c) ‚tu, Alone, single.
狂 ‚K‘wang, Mad, foolish, sport.
犬 ’Chiuen, A dog.
獅 ‚Shi, A lion.
狀 Chwang‘, Form, a lawyer‘s brief.

狹 ,Hia, (c) ,hia, Narrow stupid.
獵 Lie̍, Catch, hunt.

95. 玄

率 ,Shwai̍, Lead, imitate, all.
茲 ,Tsi̍, This, it.
玄 ,Hiuen, ,yuen, Sombre, mysterious.

96. 玉

王 ,Wan,g King, prince.
理 ,Li̍, A principle, to govern.
瑟 ,She̍, A harp of many strings.
環 ,Hwan, A ring, circle, around.
班 ,Pan, Class, to distribute.
玉 ,Ü̍, Gem, jade.
琴 ,C'hin, Harp, lute.
珍 ,Chen, Pearl.
球 ,C'hieu, Globe.
璣 ,Chi, An astronomical instrument.
玩 ,Wan̍, Joy, amusement.
玷 ,Tien̍, A flaw.
珥 ,Ri̍, Ear ring, pendant.
珠 ,Chu, Pearl, jewel.
璧 ,Pi̍, A precious gem.
珩 ,Heng, Emerald.

瑚 ,Hu, Coral.
琳 ,Lin, A kind of precious stone.
瑯 ,Lang, Neck ornaments.
琥 ,Hu, Amber.
玖 ,C'hieu, Ebony.
璀 ,Tsui̍, Lustre of a gem.
璨 ,Tsan̍, Sparkling.
瑞 ,Jui̍, Auspicious.

97. 瓜

瓜 ,Kwa, A melon.

98. 瓦

瓦 ,Wa, Tile, earthen ware.

99. 甘

甚 ,Shen̍ (c) ,shen, Intense, excessive.
甘 ,Kan, Sweet, willing.

100. 生

生 ,Sheng, Life to impart life; produce.
產 ,C'han, To give birth, an estate.
甦 ,Su, To revive.

101. 用

用 ,Yung̍, Use.

102. 田

,I̱, Different, strange.

‚Tang, tang‛, Ought, proper, in, on.

‚Yeu, From, out of.

‚Shen, Extend, repeat.

‚T‛ien, Field.

‚Nan, A male, a son.

Chie‛, Boundary.

Hü‛, c‛hü‛, Cattle, to breed.

Pi̱‛, (c) ‚pi, Ended, finished.

‚Lieu, Detain, delay.

Chia‛, ’chia, Mail, a cyclic character, the first.

Wei‛, Fear, reverence.

Lio‛, liau‛, Brief, compendious.

‚Cheu, Class, sort, field.

‚Fan, Footstep, change, times of repetition, foreign.

Pi̱‛, Give, bestow.

‚Chiang, Bound, limit.

Hwa‛, Painting, a pen stroke.

’Mu, A mow, 7260 sq. ft.

103. 疋

’P‛i, A piece of cloth.

‚I̱, Doubt, used, also for 擬 to determine.

‚Shu, Herbs, open, coarse.

’C‛hu, Pain, grief.

104. 疒

Ping‛, Sickness.

Chi̱‛, (c) ‚chi, Malady.

T‛ung‛, (c) ‚t‛ung, Pain.

‚Hen, A shade, a scar.

105. 癶

‚Teng, Ascend.

Fu‛ (c) ‚fu, Raise, start, produce.

106. 白

Pa‛ (c) ‚po, ’pai, A hundred.

‚Chie, All.

Po‛ (c) ‚pai, White.

‚Hwang, Greatest, emperor.

Ti̱‛ ’ti (c) ‚ti, Target, exact, a particle.

107. 皮

‚P‛i, Skin.

108. 皿

I̱‛, More, advantage.

Sheng‛ ‚cheng, Full, abundant.

盈 ₍Ying,₎ Full, overflowing.
盡 Chin⁽, Exhaust, finish, altogether.
監 Chien⁽, Note, survey.
盍 Ho⁽, Why not?
皿 'Min, Vessel, instrument.
盜 Tau⁽, Rob.
盟 ₍Meng,₎ Alliance.
盤 ₍P'an,₎ Dish, board.
盪 Tang⁽, A tub, large, enlarge.

109. 目

眞 ₍Chen,₎ True.
督 Tu⁽ (c) ₍tu,₎ Supervise.
眾 Chung⁽, Many.
目 Mu⁽, Eye.
眷 Chiuen⁽, A relative, to protect.
直 Chi⁽ (c) ₍chi,₎ Straight.
置 Chï⁽(c)₍chi,₎ Locate, dispose of.
省 'Hing ⁾sheng, Examine, spare, province.
看 ₍K'an, k'an⁽,₎ Look, see.
眼 'Yen, Eyes.
瞽 'Ku, Blind.
瞶 Kwei⁽, Blind.
瞻 ₍Chan,₎ Look at.

矚 ⁾Shu, Observe intently.
眠 ₍Mien,₎ Slumber.
睡 Shui⁽, Sleep.
瞬 Shun⁽, Wink of an eye.
盼 P⁽an⁽, Look, hope.
睇 Tï⁽, A glance.

110. 矛

矛 ₍Mau,₎ Spear.
務 Wu⁽, Business, earnestly.
矜 ₍Chin,₎ Boast, admire, pity.

111. 矢

知 ₍Chi,₎ Know.
矢 Shï⁽, Arrow, an oath.
短 'Toan, Short.
矧 'Shen, How much more.

112. 石

石 Shï⁽ (c) ₍shi,₎ Stone.
破 P⁽o⁽, Break, burst, open,
磐 P₍an,₎ A broad, rock.
磨 Mo (c) ₎mo, A milstone.
硫 ₍Lieu,₎ Sulphur.
磬 C⁽hing⁽, A stone bell or cymbal.
碼 Ma, Cornelian, a yard, numerical figures.

VOCABULARY.

碯 *Nau*, Agate, cornelian.

砥 '*Wu*, A fine stone, but not a gem.

砆 ,*Fu*, A stone, a false gem.

確 *C'hio'*, Solid, real, reliable.

113. 示

神 ,*Shen*, God, spirit.

祭 *Chi'*, Sacrifice, offering.

福 *Fu'*, (c) ,*fu*, Happiness.

禮 '*Li*, Rites, politeness, propriety.

視 *Shi'*, To view, to treat.

禁 *Chin'*, Prohibit.

祝 *Chu'*, ,*chu*, Bless, pray.

祈 ,*C'hi*, Pray, beg.

禱 '*tau*, Supplicate, Pray.

禍 *Hwo'*, Misery. calamity.

示 *Shi'*, Show, inform, a manifesto.

祖 '*Tsu*, Grandfather, ancestor.

祜 '*Hu*, Bliss, prosperity.

祀 *Si'*, Sacrifice, offering.

禦 '*Ü*, Withstand, resist.

祥 ,*Siang*, Prosperity, luck.

114. 禸

禽 ,*C'hin*, Fowls, birds.

115. 禾

禾 ,*Ho*, Growing rice.

穌 ,*Su*, Revive, *Yesu*, Jesus.

稱 ,*Cheng c'heng'*, Praise, address, weigh, fit.

穀 *Ku'* (c) ,*ku*, Grain.

私 ,*Si*, Private, selfish.

種 *Chung'* ,*chung*, Plant, kind, sort.

稽 ,*Chi*, Search, examine.

秉 '*Ping*, Hold fast, adhere, handful.

積 *Chi'* (c) ,*chi*, Collect, store up.

稅 *Shui'*, Taxes, duties.

穢 *Wei'*, Filth.

移 ,*I*, Move, change.

秘 ,*Pi*, Secret.

程 ,*C'heng*, Road, journey.

秋 ,*C'hieu*, Autumn.

廩 '*Lin*, Store house.

穩 '*Yin*, Firm, secure.

秦 ,*C'hin*, Name of a dynasty.

秀 *Hieu'*, Bloom, flourish, elegant.

穆 *Mu'*, Sublime, benign.

116. 穴

穴 *Hiue'* ,*hiue*, Cave, tomb.

空 ‚Kung kung‚, Empty.
竄 'Chün, Persecute.
窮 ‚Chiung, Exhaust, poor.
竊 Chie‚, Steal, stealthy.
穹 ‚Chiung, Lofty, canopy of heaven.
突 Tu‚ (c) ‚tu, Sudden, rush.
究 ‚Chieu, Search out.
窻 ‚Ch'wang, Window.
窺 ‚K'wei, Pry, spy.

117. 立

立 Li‚, Stand.
章 ‚Chang, Chapter, display.
端 ‚Toan, Correct, an item, commencement.
童 ‚T'ung, Boy, maiden.
竭 Chie‚ (c) ‚chie, Exhaust, complete.
竟 Ching‚, Finally.
竚 Chu‚, Stand, cause to stand.
競 Ching‚, Strive, earnest.

118. 竹

第 Ti‚, Number, mansion, only.
等 'Teng, Class, equal, &c.
節 Chie‚ (c) Chie, Joint, verse.
築 Chu‚, Found, build.
答 Ta‚ (c) ‚Ta, Answer.
篇 ‚P'ien, Essay, chapter, section.
笑 Hiau‚, Laugh, smile.
簡 'Chien, Brief, convenient.
筵 ‚Yen, Feast, invite.
篤 'Tu, Real, sincere.
管 'Kwan, Govern.
算 Soan‚, Estimate, calculate.
簪 ‚Tsen (c) ‚Tsan, Hairpin.
筯 Chu‚, Chopstick.
筆 'Pi, Pencil.
竹 Chu‚ (c) ‚chu, Bamboo.
簫 ‚Hiau, Flute, flageolet.
竽 ‚Ü, Piper.

119. 米

米 'Mi, Rice.
精 ‚Ching, Essence, fine, accurate.
粗 ‚Ts'u, Coarse.
糧 ‚Liang, Provender.
粉 'Fen, Starch, flour.

120. 糸

約 Yo‚, (c) ‚yo, Agreement, narrow, sparing.

素 Su‘, Plain, unadorned, ordinary, hitherto.
細 Hi‘, Fine, small.
緣 ‚Yuen, Because, therefore, a hidden harmony.
終 ‚Chung, End, final, not at all.
結 Chie‘, (c) ‚chie, Tie, connect.
維 ‚Wei, Connect, only, merely.
總 ‚Tsung, Generally, altogether.
統 ’T‘ung, Entire, general.
絕 Chiue‘, (c) ‚chiue, Cut off, extinguish.
紀 Chi‘, Period of 12 years, a record.
經 ‚Ching, Rule, classic, warp, longitude, experience.
編 ‚Pien, To twine, compose verses or books.
納 Na‘, Pay, give, receive.
給 Chi‘, (c) ’chi, ’kei, Give.
綱 ‚Kang, Main principles.
綿 ‚Mien, Floss, cottony silk, extended, connected.
縱 ‚Tsung, ’tsung, tsung‘, Let loose suppose, a direct line.
繼 Chi‘, To succeed, connect with.
繁 ‚Fan, Numerous, abundant.

純 ‚C‘hun, Pure sincere, perfect.
網 ’Wang, A net.
紅 ‚Hung, Red.
綻 Ts‘an‘, chan, A rip, rent, hole.
索 ’So, so‘, A cord, to seek.
繫 Hi‘, Tie, bind.
系 Hi‘, Family line, connect.
緯 ’Wei, Transverse, woof, latitude.
緬 Mien‘, Fine threads, connected thought, ponder.
繚 ‚Liau, ⎰ Wind around, environ, saunter.
繞 ’Jau, ⎱
縷 ’Lü, A filament, a nice distinction.
締 T‘i‘, Indissolubly joined, adapted.
帛 ‚Mien, Floss, extended, connected.
綺 ’C‘hi, Silk gauze.
絺 ‚Chi, Grass cloth.
綌 ‚Hi, Hemp cloth.
繡 Hieu‘, Embroider, decorate.
絲 ‚Si, Silk thread, raw silk.
綠 Lu‘, (c) lü‘, Green.
累 ’Lei, Often, entangle.

織 Chi‘, (c) ‚chi, Weave.
組 ’Tsu, Fringe, tape, badge of office.
紬 ‚C‘heu, Draw threads for weaving, silk, pongee.
繹 I‘, Draw out, unravel, long, utmost.
緝 Chi‘, Twist, join, continue, compose; pursue, seize.

121. 缶

缺 C‘hiue‘,(c)‚chiue, Deficit, gap, few.

122. 网

罪 Tsui‘, Sin, guilt.
羅 ‚Lo, A net, gauze.
罕 ’Han, Rare, admire.
罰 Fa‘ (c) ‚fa, Punish, fine.
罹 ‚Lo ‚li, Encounter.
署 Shu‘ (c) ‚shu, Yamun, office, manage, act pro tempore.
罔 ’Wang, Without, privative.

123. 羊

羊 ‚Yang, Sheep, goat.
羣 ‚Ch‘ün, Herd.
義 I‘, Justice, righteousness, kindness, friendship, patriotism.
美 ’Mei, Beautiful.

羔 ‚Kau, Lamb.
羞 ‚Hieu, Shame.
羨 Hien‘, Covet, long for.
羶 ‚Shan, Fetid, rank odor.

124. 羽

翰 Hau‘, A quill.
翼 I‘, Wing, aid.
習 Hi‘ (c) ‚hi, Repeat, imitate, learn.
翦 ’Chien, Destroy.
翠 Ts‘ui‘, A green bird.
耀 Yo‘ yau‘, Splendor.
翕 Hi‘, Unite, combine.
翥 ’Chu, To soar.
翔 ‚Hiang, Gyrate.
翱 ‚Ngau, Hover.
翹 ‚Ch‘iau, High, raise the head.

125. 老

者 ’Che, A relative ref. to persons and things.
老 ’Lau, Old, aged.
耆 ‚C‘hi, Aged, an elder.
耈 ’Keu, Superannuated wrinkled.

126. 而

而 ‚Ri, And, but.

崞 ,Chwen, Solely, bent on.
耐 ,Nai‘, Patience perseverance.

127. 耒
耕 ,Keng, Plow.

128. 耳
耳 'Ri, Ear, a euphonic.
聖 ,Sheng‘, Sacred, sage, holy.
聽 ,T‘ing t‘ing‘, Hear, allow.
聞 ,Wen, Hear, perceive.
耶 ,Ya (e) ye, Interrogative final, Ye su, Jesus.
聲 ,Sheng, Sound, report.
聚 ,Chü‘, Collect.
聰 ,Tsung, Wise, quickeared.
職 ,Chĭ (c) ,chi, Office.
聾 ,Lung, Deaf.
聯 ,Lien, Unite.

129. 聿
肇 ,Chau‘, Strike, commence.
肅 ,Su‘, Respectful.
肄 ,I‘, Practice, assiduous.

130. 肉
能 ,Neng, Able, can.
肉 ,Jü‘ (c) ,jeu‘, Flesh.
脫 ,T‘o‘ (c) ,to‘, Extricate.

膏 ,Kau, Grease, anoint.
背 ,Pei‘, Back, carry on the back, turn the back, recite.
胎 ,T‘ai, The womb.
育 ü‘, Rear, nurture.
肯 ’K‘en, Willing.
胜 ,Fei, Leg bones.
肥 ,Fei, Fat.
膽 ’Tan, Gall, courage.
腹 ’Fu, Bosom, belly.
膚 ,Fu, Skin.
胞 ,Pau, Womb.
胚 ’P‘i, Conception.
臚 ,Lu, Order, record.
脂 ,Chĭ, Fat, essence.
胡 ,Hu, Why? Northern barbarians.
腥 ,Hing, A fishy odor.
肴 ,Yau, Meats, viands.
臠 ,Loan, ,loan, Minced meat.
腐 ’Fu, Decayed, rotten.
胥 ,Hü, Altogether, almost.

131. 臣
臣 ,C‘hen, Officer, liege.
臨 ,Lin, Arrive, confront.

卧 Woʻ, Slumber.

132. 自

自 Tsïʻ, Self, of course, from.
臭 Hieuʻ (c) cʻheuʻ, Smell, decay.

133. 至

至 Chïʻ, Arrive at, most.
到 Tauʻ, To, at, arrive.
臺 ‚Tai, Terrace, stage.
臻 ‚Chen, Arrive, extend, in the highest degree.

134. 臼

與 ‚Ü, With, give, interrogative?
舊 Chieuʻ, Old, ancient.
興 ‚Hing, Rise, raise, flourish.
舁 ‚Ü, Bear aloft, sustain.

135. 舌

舍 She, Cottage, yield, give up.

137. 舟

舟 ‚Cheu, Ship, vessel.
船 ‚Chʻwen, Boat, ship.

138. 艮

良 ‚Liang, Good, virtuous, rather
艱 ‚Chien, Difficult.

139. 色

色 Seʻ shoʻ (c) ʼshai, Color, beauty, amorous.

140. 艸

萬 Wanʻ, A myriad, all.
若 Joʻ, If, suppose, like, that, his, its.
蓋 Kaiʻ, Because, cover.
華 ‚Hwa ‚hwa, Flower, glory.
蒙 ‚Meng, ʼmeng, Simple, cover, receive favor.
苦 ʼKʻu, Bitter.
莽 Tsangʻ, Inter.
蓮 ‚Lien, Water lily.
蘭 ‚Lan, A flower, Aglaia odorata.
藏 ‚Tsʻang, tsangʻ, Conceal, store.
荒 ‚Hwang, Wild, waste, barren.
莫 Moʻ, No, not, must not.
英 ‚Ying, Bloom, brave, heroic.
花 ‚Hwa, Flower.
藉 Chieʻ, Reliance, pretext, record.
葡 ‚Pʻu. } Grape.
萄 ‚Tau.
著 Choʻ chuʻ, An affix expressive of completion, to send, publish, display.

落 Loʻ (c) luw, Fall.
苟 ʼKeu, If, doubtful, irregular.
蒼 ‚Tsang, Azure.
薄 Poʻ (c) ‚pau, Thin.
護 Poʻ (c) ‚pau, Protect.
荷 Hoʻ ‚ho, Lotus, to bear, receive favor.
蔽 Pi, Veil, to obscure.
藐 ʼMiau, Minute, slight.
藥 Yoʻ (c) yau, Medecine.
蕪 ʼFu, ‚wu, Weeds, rubbish.
薨 ʼHung, Death of a noble.
菓 ‚Kwo, Fruits.
葉 Yeʻ, Leaves.
蘇 ‚Su, Cheerful, also 穌 to revive.
草 ʼTsau, Grass.
苗 ‚Miau, Germ, aboriginal.
茂 Mawʻ, meuʻ, Flourishing, abundant.
薦 Chienʻ, Recommend.
葛 ʼKo (c) ‚ko, Flax.
蔭 Yinʻ, Shade.
苑 Yuenʻ, Pasture, park, luxuriant.
芳 ‚Fang, Fragrance.

藝 Iʻ, Plant, cultivate, craft, art.
蓄 Hüʻ, Nourish, hoard.
菜 Tsʻaiʻ, Herbs.
薇 ‚Wei, Pot herbs.
葵 ‚Kwʻei, Malvaceous plants, the sunflower.
芥 Chieʻ, Mustard.
芬 ‚Fen, Perfume of opening flowers.
蕩 Tangʻ, Vagrant, vast.
蕃 Luxuriant.

141. 疒

處 ʼCʻhu, Cʻhuʻ, Place, dwell.
虛 ‚Hü, Empty, vain.
號 Hawʻ, Sign, title, cry.
虔 ‚Cʻhien, Earnest, devout.
虐 Nioʻ, (c) niauʻ, Oppress, injure.
虜 ʼLo, Prisoner, ravage.

142. 虫

蛇 ‚She, Serpent.
蜜 Miʻ, Honey.
蟲 ‚Cʻhung, Insect, worm.
蠻 ‚Man, Savage.
螺 ‚Lo, A Small sea shell.

蝗 ˏHwang, Locust.
蝦 ˏHia, Shrimp, crawfish.
蛤 ʼKo (c) ˏko, Oyster, muscle.
蠶 ˏTʻsan, Silk worm.
蛛 ˏChu, Spider.
蚓 ʼYin, Earthworm.
蟬 ˏCʻhan, A kind of locust.
蟻 Iʻ, Ants.
蠅 ˏYing, Flies.

143. 血
血 Blood.

144. 行
行 ˏHing, Hang, Walk, act, hong.
街 ˏChie, Street.
衛 Weiʻ, Protect, defend.
術 Shuʻ, Method.
衢 ˏCʻhü, Street, road.
衡 ˏHeng, Transverse.
衍 ʼYen, Inundate, amplify.
衒 ˏHiuen, Brag, boast, display, for 眩 to dazzle.

145. 衣
衣 ˏI, Clothes.
初 ˏCʻhu, Beginning.

被 Peiʻ, Receive, prefix to passive verbs.
裔 ˏI, Posterity.
哀 ˏAi, Grief, sorrow melancholly.
襲 Hiʻ, (c) ˏhi, Lurk, take by surprise, hereditary.
衷 ˏChung, Heart, nature.
製 Chiʻ, Manufacture.
衰 ˏShwai, Decay.
袍 ˏPʻau, Mantle robe.
囊 ˏNang, Bag, sack, yesterday.
補 ʼPu, Patch, mend.
表 ʼPiau, Outside, display, example.
裸 ʼLo, Naked.
裳 ˏCʻhang, Clothes, lower garments.
複 Fuʻ, Repeated, double.
裘 ˏCʻhieu, Jacket, vest.
裙 ˏChin, Skirt.
袖 Hieuʻ, Sleeve.
裝 ˏChwang, Adorn, repair, lade a ship.
裁 ˏTsʻai, Cut, trim, shear.
裂 Lieʻ, Rend, tear.

146. 西

西 ,Hi, West.
要 Yaw̔, Wish, will, important.
覆 Fu̔, Reply, repeat.
覈 Ho̔, Investigate, search, verify, distinguish.

147. 見

見 Chien̔, hien̔, See, be seen, appear.
親 ,C'hin, Kindred, intimacy, self, own.
現 Hien̔, At present, appear.
觀 ,Kwan, Behold, consider.
覺 Chio̔, (c) chiau̔, Conscious, feel, awake.
覩 Tu̔, Look, see.
覲 Chin̔, Interview with a superior.
覿 Ti̔, See, face to face.
覓 Mi̔, Seek.

148. 角

角 Chio̔, (c) ,chiau, Horn, corner.
解 'Chie, Untie, explain.
觚 ,Hu, ,ku, Square, law, plan, a square vessel, a wine cup.

149. 言

言 ,Yen, Words, speak.
謂 Wei̔, Say, call.
諸 ,Chu, Many, all, plural prefix, in, at.
訓 Hün̔, Instruct.
詳 ,Hiang, Full, minute, in detail.
譬 P'i̔, Compare, parable.
試 Shi̔, Try, endeavor.
諭 U̔, Edict, command.
誡 Chie̔, Ordinance, commandment.
謀 ,Mu, ,meu, Plan, plot.
該 ,Kai, Ought, altogether, the said.
謝 Hie̔, To thank, to decline.
許 'Hü, Promise, intensive particle.
詛 'Tsu, Curse, imprecation.
請 'C'hing, Invite, request, inquire.
讚 Tsan̔, Praise.
記 Chi̔, Record, remember.
誠 ,C'heng, Sincere, honest.
證 Cheng̔, Evidence, witness.
語 'Ü, Words, discourse.
詣 I̔, Visit.
說 Shwo̔, (c) ,shwo, Speak, nar- [rative.

計 Chì, Count, calculate.
誰 ₂Shui, Who?
讓 Jang⁽, Yield, relinquish.
論 Lun⁽ ₂lun, Discourse, treatise.
誓 Shi⁽, Oath, swear.
識 Shi⁽, (c) ₂shi, Know, remember.
議 I⁽, Discuss, negotiate.
變 Pien⁽, Turn, change.
訟 Sung⁽, Accuse, law suit.
詞 ₂Ts⁽z, Words, verses, statement.
託 T⁽o⁽, (c) ₂t⁽o, Entrust, pretend.
詔 Chau⁽, Summon.
誘 Yeu⁽, Win, beguile, persuade.
誨 Hwei⁽, Instruct, admonish.
謳 ₂Ngeu, Recite, sing.
誦 Sung⁽, Read, recite.
詩 ₂Shi, Verses, poetry.
講 ⁾Chiang, Speak, discourse.
誕 Tan⁽, Birth, advent of a great man, great, false.
譴 ⁾Chien, Rebuke, punish.
詭 ⁾Kwei, Deceit.
謙 ⁾C⁽hien, Modest.

讀 Tu⁽, (c) ₂tu, Read.
認 Jen⁽, Recognize, acknowledge.
誇 Kw⁽a, Boast.
詰 Chie⁽, Inquire.
謹 ⁾Chin, Careful, respectful.
譽 ₂Ü, Praise.
謗 Pang⁽, Slander.
誤 Wu⁽, Mistake, error.
謬 Mieu⁽, Error.
調 ₂T⁽iau, tiau⁽, Turn, temper, mix.
辯 Pien⁽, Eloquent, distinguish, vindicate.
訝 Ya⁽, Frightened, astonished.
諂 ⁾C⁽han, Flattery.
譏 ₂Chi, Ridicule.
評 ₂P⁽ing, Censure, criticism.
詠 ⁾Yung, Sing.
諧 ₂Hie, Harmony.
詎 Chü⁽, Who? How?
譜 ⁾Pu, Record, catalogue.
諏 ₂Tseu, Consult, inquire.
警 ⁾Ching, Warn, caution, exhort to respect.

150. 谷
谷 Ku‘, (c) ?ku, Valley.

151. 豆
豈 ’Chi, How?
豐 ,Feng, Opulent.
豔 Yen‘, Beauty.

152. 豕
象 ,Hiang, Elephant, ivory.
豳 ,Pin, Name of a state.
豚 ,T‘un, A pig.
豪 ,Hau, Rich, opulent.
豫 ü‘, Beforehand, doubt, suspicion, luxury.

153. 豸
貌 Mu‘, Appearance.
貊 Mo‘, Barbarian.

154. 貝
賜 Si (c) t‘si‘, Bestow, confer.
贖 Shu‘ (c) ‚Shu, Redeem.
負 Fu‘, Bear on the back, turn the back.
責 Che‘ (c) ‚tse, Rebuke, reprove.
財 ‚Tsai, Riches.
貴 Kwei‘, Honorable.
賽 Sai‘ se‘, Vie, display.

貧 P‘in, Poor, impoverished.
貨 Ho‘, Goods..
賦 Fu‘, Conferred by heaven.
質 Chi‘, Talent, matter.
貪 ‚T‘an, Covet.
買 ’Mai, Buy.
賣 Mai‘, Sell.
貢 Kung‘, Tribute.
賢 ‚Hien, Worthy, wise.
賓 ‚Pin, Guest, retainer.
賞 ’Shang, Reward.
賊 Tse‘ (c) ‚tsei, Thief, steal, injure.
資 ‚Tsi, Means, rely on.
貯 Chu‘, Hoard, store up.
賡 ‚Keng, Repeat a song, join, continue.

155. 赤
赦 She‘, Forgive.
赤 Ch‘i‘, Red, sincere.
赫 Ho‘, Awful, majestic.

156. 走
越 Yue‘, Pass, leap over.
起 ’Ch‘i, Rise, raise.
走 ’Tseu, Walk, run.

趨 ,Chʻü, Run,
赴 Fuʻ, Go.
趁 Chʻenʻ, Follow, improve opportunity.

157. 足

路 Luʻ, Road, way.
足 Tsuʻ (c) ₄tsu, Foot, enough.
踐 Chienʻ, Tread.
蹟 Chiʻ, Track.
跪 Kweiʻ, Kneel.
蹈 ₂Tau, Tread, stamp.
蹠 Chiʻ, Going back and forth.
躅 ₄Chʻü chuʻ, Walk, unsteady.
蹙 ₄Chu, Hastily overleaping, hesitating.
躊 ₄Chʻeu, Undecided.
躋 Chiʻ, Cling, climb, rise.
跳 Tʻiauʻ, Leap.
躍 Yoʻ, Spring, dance.
跣 ʼHi, Barefoot.
跪 Kweiʻ, Kneel.
踧 Tsuʻ, Walk circumspectly.
蹐 Chiʻ, Walk with measured steps, reverently.

158. 身

身 ₂Shen, Body, person.
躬 ₂Kung, Person, self.
軀 ₂Chʻü, Body, person.

159. 車

車 ₂Chʻü ₂chʻe, Wagon, chariot.
較 Chiauʻ, Compare.
軍 ₂Chiün, Army.
轄 Hiaʻ (c) ₄hia, Control.
載 Tsaiʻ, Convey, a year.
輕 ₂Chʻing, Light.
輩 Peiʻ, Class, grade.
輪 ₄Lun, Wheel.
輸 ₂Shu, Rotate, pay out, lose, be beaten.
轉 ʼChwen, chwenʻ, Turn.
輝 ₂Hwei, Splendor, lustre.
輿 ₄Ü, Imperial domain.
輻 ʼFu, Spokes of a wheel, with next to collect.
轂 ₂Tʻseu, Hub of a wheel.
輔 ₂Fu, Aid.
轟 ₂Hung, Booming, as of cannon.

160. 辛

幸 Hingʻ, Fortunate.
辜 ₂Ku, Offence, guilt.
辭 Tʻsi, Words, to decline.

辨 Pien, Distinguish.
辛 ,Hin, Bitter, acrid.

161. 辰

辱 Ju͑, Shame, disgrace.
農 ,Nung, Husbandman.
辰 ,Chen, Time, the 5th hour.

162. 辵

遂 ,Sui, Then, thereon, at once.
迦 ,Chia, A name of Budha.
道 Tau͑, Way, method, truth, doctrine, reason.
過 Kwo͑, Pass, cross over, transgress.
逃 ,Tau, Escape, fly.
選 ʼHiuen, Select, choose.
追 ,Chui, Pursue.
造 Tsau͑, Create, make.
遠 ʼYuen, Far, long.
避 Pi͑, Avoid, escape.
迨 Tai͑, Until.
返 ʼFan, Return.
適 Shi͑, Meet, suit, go.
遺 ,I, Omit, transmit, let fall, leave behind.
遵 ,Tsun, Observe, obey.
遣 ʼChien, Send.

違 ,Wei, Oppose, withdraw from.
逆 Ni͑, Contrary, resist.
遭 ,Tsau, Meet, encounter.
途 ,Tu, Path, road.
遍 Pien͑, Everywhere.
速 Su͑ (c) ,su, Hasten.
通 ,Tung, Open, reasonable.
達 Ta͑ (c) ,ta, Open, intelligent, prosperous.
逐 Chu͑, Eject, persecute.
近 Chin͑, Near.
邀 ,Yau, Invite.
述 Shu͑, (c) ,shu, Narrate, relate.
進 Chin͑, Enter.
迫 Po͑ p'o͑, Urge.
迷 ,Mi, Delude, astray.
遐 ,Hia, hia͑, Remote.
邇 ʼRi, Near.
巡 ,Chwen, ,'wen, Go and come, haste.
遊 ,Yeu, Roam, rove.
運 Yün͑, Revolve, circulate, transport.
還 ,Hwan, Return.
連 ,Lien, Connect, together.
迎 ,Ying, Meet, welcome.

遷 ,C‘hien, Remove.
送 Sung, Present, send away.
遁 Tun‘, Escape.
退 T‘ui‘, Retire.
逾 ,Ü, Leap over, surpass.
遜 Hiün‘, Yielding, modest.
迄 ‘C‘hi, End, finish.
迹 Chi‘, Footstep.
迅 Hiün‘, Vivid, energetic.
逝 Shi‘, Passing, vanishing.
遽 Chü‘, Suddenly.
迢 ,T‘iau, Distant, remote.
遞 Ti‘, Transmit, distant.
遴 ,Lin, Elect, covetous, mean.
迓 Ya‘, Meet, welcome, invite.
遑 ,Hwan, Liesure, vacant.
逸 I‘, Pleasure, escape.
遨 ,Ngau, ,ngau, Roam, saunter.
邃 Sui‘, In the rear, far back, as a suite of rooms.

逢 ,Feng, Meet.
邊 ,Pien, Side, border.

163. 邑

邑 I‘, City, district.

鄉 ,Hiang, Village, neighborhood, the country.
邦 ,Pang, Nation, state.
都 ,Tu, Capital city.
郊 ,Chiau, Suburban fields.
却 C‘hio‘, Reject, forsooth, also.
那 Na‘ ,na, That, how, where?
郇 ,Hiün, Name of a place, Zion.
邪 ,Hie, Oblique, perverse, corrupt.
部 Pu‘, Class, sort, bureau, board, volume.
鄰 ,Lin, Neighbor.

164. 酉

醫 ,I, Heal.
醒 ‘Hing, ,hing, Awake.
酬 ,C‘heu, Reciprocate, friendly intercourse.
釁 Hin‘, Fault, defect quarrel.
酵 Kiau‘, Leaven, yeast.
配 P‘ei‘, Unite, fit together.
釀 ‘Niang, Ferment.
酣 ,Han, Intoxicate.
酸 ,Soan, Sour.

165. 釆

釋 Shi, Loose, release expound, protect, Budha.

166. 里

里 'Li, Neighborhood, Chinese mile, 1897¼ Eng. ft, in geography, 1460¼ ft, $\frac{1}{250}$ of a deg.

野 'Ye, Pasture, wilderness.

重 Chung‘ ‚chung, Heavy, double, again.

量 ‚Liang, liang‘, Measure.

167. 金

金 ‚Chin, Gold, metal.
錫 Hi‘ (c) ‚hi, Tin, bestow.
錄 Lu‘, Record.
銀 ‚Yin, Silver.
銅 ‚T‘ung, Copper, brass.
鐵 ’T‘ie, Iron.
鑑 Chien‘, Mirror.
鑒 Chien‘, Inspect, oversee.
鑄 Chu‘, Cast, found, manufacture.
錢 ‚Chien, Cash, money.
釘 ‚Ting, Nail.
鋒 ‚Feng, Point, edge.
錯 Tso‘, Mistake, scattered.
鑿 Tso‘ (c) ‚tsau, Bore, chisel.
鐲 Cho‘, (c) ‚cho, Bracelet.

鐶 ‚Hwan, Ring.
錦 ’Chin, Gilding, brocade.
鑲 ‚Hiang, Border, inlaid.
鐘 ‚Chung, Bell, clock.
鑪 ‚Lu, Furnace.
鏘 ‚Chiang, A tinkling-ring.
鏗 ‚K‘eng, Ringing, jingling sound.
鈴 ‚Ling, A small bell.
鍾 ‚Chung, To love, a measure, goblet.
鈞 ‚Chiün, Equal, just, arbiter, creator, venerable.

168. 長

長 ’Chang, ‚Chang, Elder, superior, long.

169. 瓜

門 ‚Men, Gate, door.
闢 P‘i‘, Open.
間 Chien‘ ‚chien, In, between.
開 ‚K‘ai, Open.
閉 Pi‘, Shut.
閃 ’Shan, Dart.
闊 K‘o‘, Wide.
閱 Yue‘, Look over, pass over.
閣 Ko‘ (c) ‚ko, Gallery.

開 ₍Hien, Vacant.

170. 阜

降 Chiang⟨ ⸜hiang, Come down, send down, degrade surrender.
隱 'Yin, Hide, conceal.
陳 ₍Chen, Display, arrange, order of battle.
陷 Hien⟨, Fall into, entrap.
隨 ⸜Sui, Follow, at option.
阿 ⸜Ngo ⸜ngo, Cringe, flatter, lean on, partial, prefix to names.
陰 ⸜Yin, The dark, or female principle.
除 ₍Chu, Exclude, besides.
隅 ⸜Ü, Corner.
際 Chi⟨, Limit, border, junction.
阻 'Tsu, Obstacle, hinder.
陸 Lu⟨, Dry land, by land.
隙 Hi⟨, A quarrel, cranny.
防 ₍Fang, Guard against.
院 Yuen⟨, Court, hall, office.
附 'Fu (c) ⸜fu, Append.
險 ⸜Hien, Steep, perilous.
陞 Chi⟨, Climb, promotion.
限 Hien⟨, Limit.

172. 隹

雅 'Ya, Refined, literary.
難 ₍Nan nan⟨, Hard, difficult.
離 ₍Li, Leave.
雖 ⸜Sui, ⸜sui, Though.
雜 Tsa⟨ (c) ⸜tsa, Mixed, promiscuous.
雙 ⸜Shwang, Double, a pair.
雕 ⸜Tiau, Carve, adorn, tattoo.
雞 ₍Chi, Chicken.
雀 Chio⟨ (c) 'chiau, Sparrow.
雍 ⸜Yung, Harmony.

173. 雨

靈 ₍Ling, Spirit, intelligent, effectual.
雨 'Ü, Rain.
雲 ₍Yün, Clouds.
震 Chen⟨, Quake, convulse.
雪 Hiue⟨, (c) hiue, Snow.
露 Lu⟨, Dew.
需 ₍Hü, Need, must.
零 ₍Ling, Scattering, remnant.
霄 ⸜Hiau, A halo, fleecy clouds, heaven.
霞 ₍Hia, Glow of sunset.
霓 ₍Ni, Rainbow.

雷 ₂Lui, Thunder.
霜 ₂Shwang, Frost.
霪 ₂Yin, Excessive rains.
霹靂 ₂T'ing, Sharp thunder.
電 Tien⁴, Lightning.

174. 青
青 ₂C'hing, Green.
靜 Ching⁴, Still, silent.
眚 ʼSheng, Fault, crime, meagre, reduce.

175. 非
非 ₂Fei, Not, is not, wrong.
靡 ₂Mi, Profuse, not, without.

176. 面
面 Mien⁴, Face.

177. 革
革 Ko⁴, (c) ₂ko, Leather, change, dismiss.
鞠 Chŭ⁴, Judge, condemn.
韁 ₂Chiang, Bridle.

178. 韋
韞 Yün⁴, Guard, conceal.

180. 音
音 ₂Yin, Voice, sound.
響 ʼHiang, Echo.

韻 Yün⁴, Rhyme.
韶 ₂Shau, Name of an air.

181. 頁
顯 ʼHien, Reveal, display.
類 Lei⁴, Class, species.
頓 Tun⁴, Bow the head, instantly, at once.
願 Yüen⁴, Willing, desirous.
顧 Ku⁴, Look, regard.
賴 Lai⁴, Depend on.
順 Shun⁴, Obey, yield, unimpeded.
預 Ü⁴, Beforehand, prepare.
頌 Sung⁴, Praise.
須 ₂Hü, Must.
頒 ₂Pan, Distribute.
頭 ₂T'eu, Head.
領 ʼLing, Stretch the neck, receive with respect.
頂 ʼTing, Bear on the head, superlative.
顢 ₂Man ₂man, Large face.
頇 ₂Han, Bald, with the preceding, stupid.
頗 ʼP'o, Somewhat, rather.

題 ,Ti, Theme, subject.
項 ,Ching, 'ching, 100 mow, an instant.
頻 ,Pin, Incessant, urgent.
顏 Yen', Color, countenance.
頑 ,Wan, Stupid, perverse.

182. 風

風 ,Feng, Wind, custom, influence.

184. 食

食 Shi (c) ,shi, Eat, food.
餅 'Ping, Loaf, cake.
養 'Yang, Nourish.
飲 'Yin, Drink.
餘 ,Ü, Overplus.
饑 ,Chi, Hunger, dearth.
飾 Shi, Ornament.
飢 ,Chi, Hunger.
饒 ,Jau, Generous in fare, in treatment, forgive.
饔 ,Yung, Breakfast.
飧 ,Sun, Supper.
飽 'Pau, Full fed, satisfied.
飫 ,ü, Sated, filled.
饌 'Tsoan, chwen', Meats, dressed food.

饈 ,Hieu, Viands, dainties.
餌 'Ri, Pastry, bait, allurement.
飯 Fan', Boiled rice.

185. 首

首 'Sheu, Head, chief, beginning.

186. 香

香 ,Hiang, Incense.
馨 ,Hin, Fragrance.

187. 馬

馬 'Ma, Horse.
驢 'Lü, Mule.
驅 ,C'hü, Drive, expel.
駭 ,Hai, Fright.
驕 ,Chiau, Pride.
駐 Chu', Reside.
驗 Yen', Test.
駕 Chia', Equipage, the Emperor, thou.
驚 ,Ching, Fright.
騎 ,C'hi, chi', Ride, rider.
駝 ,To, Camel.
驟 Cheu', Sudden, gallop.
駛 'Shi, Sail.
驥 Chi', A fine horse.

騰 ,Teng, Mount up, run swiftly.
驊 ,Hwa, An elegant horse.
騮 ,Lieu A bay or sorrel.
馳 ,Ch'i, Run, gallop.
騁 'Ch'eng, Run swiftly.

188. 骨
體 'T'i, Body, substance, members, sympathy.
骨 'Ku (c) ,ku, Bone.

189. 高
高 ,Kau, High.

190. 髟
髮 'Fa fa', Hair.
髫 ,T'iau, Loose ringlets, young, youthful.
髦 ,Mau, Hair, eminent, courageous.

191. 鬥
鬥 ,Tew, Contend.
鬨 ,Hung', A confused noise.

192. 鬯
鬱 U', Fragrant, pent, vexed.

193. 鬲
鬻 U', Buy, sell.
融 ,Yung, Bright, harmonious.

194. 鬼
鬼 'Kwei, Ghost, devil.
魔 ,Mo, Devil, temptation.
魂 ,Hwun, Soul.

195. 魚
魚 ,U, Fish.
魯 'Lu, Stupid, name of a kingdom.
鮮 ,Hien 'hien, Fresh, rare.
鱗 ,Lin, Scales, fish.
鯤 ,Kw'un, Leviathan.
鰲 ,Au, A monster said to sustain the earth.
鯨 ,Ching, Whale.
鼉 Ngau', ngo', Alligator.

196. 鳥
鳥 ,Niau, Bird.
鴿 Ko' (c) ,ko, Dove, pigeon.
鳴 ,Ming, Cry, sound.
鳳 Feng', Phoenix.
鸞 ,Loan, Bird of paradise.
鶴 Ho' (c) ,hau, Stork, crane.
鴻 ,Hung, Wild goose.
鵲 C'hio', Magpie, daw, jay.

197. 鹵
鹽 ,Yen, Salt.

198. 鹿
麗 *Lí*, Beautiful, splendid.
麟 ʻ*Lin*, An animal, which appears at the birth of a sage.
麈 ʼ*Chu*, A deer with a bushy tail.
麤 ʻ*Tsʻu*, Coarse.

199. 麥
麥 *Moʻ* (c) *maiʻ*, Wheat.

200. 麻
麻 ʻ*Ma*, Hemp.
麼 ʼ*Mo* (c) ʻ*ma* ʼ*ma*, Minute, delicate, interrogative.

201. 黃
黃 ʻ*Hwang*, Yellow.

203. 黑
默 *Moʻ*, Silent.
黑 *Hoʻ* (c) ʻ*heiʻ*, Black.
黨 ʼ*Tang*, Clan, company.
黛 *Taiʻ*, Dark green.

205. 黽
黽 ʼ*Minʻ*, Strive, urge, a frog.
鼈 *Pieʻ*, (c) ʼ*pie*, A turtle supposed to hear with its eyes.
黿 ʻ*Yuen*, Tortoise.
鼉 ʻ*Tʻo*, A large iguana.

206. 鼎
鼎 ʼ*Ting*, A censer.

207. 鼓
鼓 ʼ*Ku*, Drum, excite.

210. 齊
齊 ʻ*Cʻhi*, Evenly, united, name of a state.
齋 ʻ*Chai*, Studio, penance.

211. 齒
齒 ʼ*Cʻhi*, Upper front teeth.
齡 ʻ*Ling*, Front teeth, sign of age.

212. 龍
龍 ʻ*Lung*, Dragon.

213. 龜
龜 ʻ*Kwei*, Tortoise.

214. 龠
籲 *Yoʻ*, Supplicate.

www.ingramcontent.com/pod-product-compliance
Lightning Source LLC
Chambersburg PA
CBHW020921230426
43666CB00008B/1519